America's Old Age Crisis

AMERICA'S OLD AGE CRISIS

*Public Policy and
the Two Worlds of Aging*

STEPHEN CRYSTAL

Basic Books, Inc., Publishers   New York

362.60973
C957a

Library of Congress Cataloging in Publication Data

Crystal, Stephen, 1946–
America's old age crisis.

Includes bibliographical references and index.
1. Aged—Government policy—United States.
2. Social security—United States. 3. Aged—Services
for—United States. 4. Aged—United States—Family
relationships. I. Title.
HQ1064.U5C79   1982   362.6'0973   82-70849
ISBN 0-465-00124-6

Contents

Acknowledgments

MANY PEOPLE helped me with this project. Mary Jo Bane, Lee Rainwater, Barbara Heyns, and Nathan Glazer, as well as James A. Davis, Tamara Hareven, Susan Radius, Paul Starr, and Ezra Vogel read and commented on the manuscript or the papers that were its predecessors. Peter Skerry, John Myles, and Joshua Wiener also discussed the issues with me.

For access to data, I am indebted to the National Opinion Research Center, the Louis Harris organization, the Roper Public Opinion Research Center, Project Impress of Dartmouth College, the Survey Research Center of the University of North Carolina, the Office of Management and Budget, the National Center for Health Statistics, the Bureau of the Census, and to Professors Rainwater and Bane. I also thank the staff of the William James computing facility at Harvard University. A research expenses grant from Harvard was helpful.

Martin Kessler, President of Basic Books, encouraged me to turn a too-long manuscript into a book addressed to a general as well as a specialist audience. Linda Carbone provided highly competent assistance at the copy-editing stage.

America's Old Age Crisis

1

The Aging Dilemma

TODAY it is widely felt that we've reached a watershed in social and economic policy. Social welfare costs seem increasingly burdensome, yet the programs are perceived as falling short of expectations. The economy appears stagnant, burdened by inadequate capital formation and economic dead weight, and there is a sense of unease about the functioning of the family and other small-scale social institutions. What is not widely appreciated is the extent to which these problems involve our policies for the care and support of the aging.

In many ways, aging policy has become a major dilemma for our society. Benefits for the aged command an increasingly large share of the budget, putting the squeeze on other programs. Yet many elderly suffer severe deprivation, and the "social safety net" fails to catch them. Despite fast-escalating costs, our benefit system is neither equitable nor efficient. Why do we seem to be spending more now but getting less for it?

Deciding what to do is all the more difficult because we are not clear about the nature of the problem or about our own objectives. There is little understanding of how existing programs actually operate, what they cost, who benefits, and how government and family interact in providing help. The changes of recent decades are not understood. There are pervasive mythologies about the elderly, their needs and their resources. In order to plan intelligently, we need to understand the current state of affairs.

Social Change and the Support of the Aged

Recent years have seen remarkable, even revolutionary changes in the economic and social relationships between the generations. In Western nations until the twentieth century, as in most of the underdeveloped world today, the majority of the population was under 25, and the person who reached 65 was a rarity. By the turn of the century, life expectancy in the United States was still only 49 years,[1] and the median age of the population was 23.[2] Four percent of the population was elderly, approximately 1.6 million elderly men and slightly fewer women. The concept of retirement really did not exist. An estimated 68 percent of men 65 and over were gainfully employed,[3] and support was commonly provided by the families of the elderly, with whom they were likely to reside.

By the late 1930s, when the Social Security system was established, the proportion of elderly had risen to about 7 percent of the population. Most of the elderly men were still in the labor force, though many were unemployed. And most still depended on their jobs, savings if any, and families. In one of its first issues, the *Social Security Bulletin* reported that 45 percent of the elderly were dependent on friends and relatives.[4]

This meant that the initial cost of the emerging system of public benefits was remarkably low. Today's problems—in particular the enormous costs, which place such heavy burdens on the working-age population and result in agonizing political choices and pressures—are relatively recent, and represent the

4

beginning of a new era in social policy. The transition from high to low fertility, the maturing of the population structure, and other dramatic demographic changes are transforming the society. Issues that were once a sideshow in social welfare, while the main events concerned working-age families and their children, now occupy center stage. Social policies which shunted the aged and their problems aside in a "gilded ghetto" become less feasible as the elderly population increases.

The Increasing Government Burden

In order to understand the dilemmas and choices we face, we must first appreciate the facts of contemporary aging. The first of these is the remarkable extent to which the system of benefits for the aging has grown.

In the eyes of the public, the prototypical consumer of social welfare would probably be a minority welfare mother. The large increases in social spending of the sixties and seventies have been widely perceived as going to the economic underclass. In fact, the bulk of these increases has gone to the aged, and to a considerable extent to the middle-class elderly.

In 1982, according to a conservative Office of Management and Budget estimate, benefits to the aged accounted for 27 percent of the entire federal budget.[5] A broader definition of such benefits would produce estimates close to one-third. And it has been projected that without any further liberalization, demographic developments alone would increase the cost of current benefits to 35 percent of the budget by 2000 and 65 percent in 2025.[6] In 1981, programs for the aged accounted for about $140 billion of the $225 billion budget of the Department of Health and Human Services, as well as substantial pieces of the budgets of other agencies ranging from the Veterans' Administration to the Department of Agriculture. Today, per capita spending on the aged at all levels of government exceeds spending for children and youth, including education costs, by more than three to one.[7]

These enormous costs for aid to the aged are a fairly new phenomenon. From 1937 to 1949, Social Security taxes were a maximum of $30 per year. The maximum tax was still only $174 by 1965, less than a tenth of the 1981 rate. The cost of financing in-kind services was equally modest compared to today's outlays. In 1960, for example, expenditures at all levels of government for nursing home care for the aged represented only about $100 million per year, about one-hundredth the level they reached just 19 years later.

What kept the burden light until quite recently was a combination of lower benefit levels, the relative youth of the population, and the fact that the group paying for benefits was constantly expanding. In Social Security, for example, coverage and taxation was constantly extended to new groups. As with a chain letter, everyone benefited at first. The newly covered groups made out well, paying in for what was often just a few years and then receiving pensions, while the rest benefited from the expanded tax base. In 1950, sixteen workers were contributing to the Social Security fund to finance the benefits of each retiree. But the ratio dropped to about 3 to 1 by 1980, and is projected to hit 2 to 1 by 2025.

Major programs to assist the aged mushroomed in the 1960s and 1970s, creating a revolution of rising expectations among the elderly and those approaching old age, and also among those who might once have felt individually responsible for their support. Social Security outlays went from $11 billion in 1960 to $138 billion in 1981.[8] Medicare, begun in the late 1960s, increased almost sevenfold between 1970 and 1982, from $7 billion to $47 billion. Although they make up only about 16 percent of those enrolled, the elderly also account for an increasing share (now about 40 percent) of Medicaid, the other major Federal health program.[9]

As direct public spending expanded, so did outlays by private systems supported, in their turn, by indirect tax subsidies. Employer contributions to private pension plans went from $180 million in 1940 and $1.75 billion in 1950 to $30 billion in 1975.[10] According to federal estimates, "tax expenditures" subsidizing private pensions grew from around $3 billion in the early 1970s to $28 billion by 1981.[11] All told, federal "tax expenditures" for pension systems and benefits for the aged approximate $50 billion annually.[12] As a result of tax changes enacted in 1981, the already enormous tax subsidies will grow by leaps and bounds in the 1980s. The extension of eligibility for Individual Retirement Accounts (IRAs) to persons covered by an employee pension plan will much expand use of these tax shelters.

Limits to Growth

Even if there were no new constraints, rates of growth like these would have to level off, given finite resources. But there *are* new constraints, important ones. Benefits for each generation of the aged come from taxes on the current work force— this is as true for Social Security as for the other programs. (The popular notion that workers draw pensions from an account built up by their own contributions to the system is inaccurate: the Social Security trust funds contain only a few months' payments). Demographic change makes it more and more difficult for the working generation to maintain and improve the levels of benefits for the retired generation.

Pressures will converge when the post-World War II baby-boom generation reaches old age, toward the end of the first quarter of the next century. This group, which will have borne historically unprecedented burdens to provide old-age benefits for its parents' generation, will probably not be able to reap the

7

same rewards for itself. Unless there is a dramatic turnabout in fertility trends, the proportion of aged in the population will reach 21 percent by 2030.[13] The cost of current benefit levels, applied to this much larger eligible population, may be difficult to sustain despite the considerable political power which the elderly will then have.

In health care, the limits of growth may be even more painful and will be reached earlier. As we shall see, a number of social trends have resulted in greatly increased demand and costs for chronic health care in particular. However, these costs are concentrated on a relatively small proportion of the aged (about 6 percent), while at least an equal number of comparably impaired elderly receive care from families or simply struggle along. Unfortunately, those among the aged most vulnerable to incapacitation—the very old and the widowed—will increase much more rapidly than the total aged population, while social trends such as the steady increase in living alone will reduce access to informal care. These trends will increase demand and collide with budget pressures.

What's Wrong with Aging Policy?

The system of benefits to the aged, which has grown so dramatically, is a remarkable mélange of programs based on varied eligibility, financing, and administrative principles. The programs reflect compromises on the fundamental issues of *who pays* and *who benefits*. These choices involve conflicting goals, interests, and principles of program design. Coalitions of diverse interests were formed around these programs during the era of growth. In the process, the distributional conflicts were often avoided, or at least not faced explicitly. But sweeping these issues under the rug becomes more and more difficult in an era of limits.

What's Wrong with Aging Policy?

The most important choices are between the better-off and worst-off groups of the elderly. Advocates of benefits to the aged often implicitly assume that the aged are a relatively homogeneous group with a common set of problems and needs. On this basis, benefits to old people—any old people—are seen as solutions to the needs of all, without further analysis of who among them really benefits. In fact, the aging inhabit two worlds, and their problems, interests, needs, and ability to articulate their needs and secure entitlements diverge sharply. The elderly who are worst-off include many of those over 75; of the widowed, single, or divorced; of those in poor health; of those without assets or income from private pensions and investments; and of those with low incomes. These attributes often cluster in patterns of "multiple jeopardy." The public policy initiatives of the sixties and seventies raised the average economic level of the aged relative to the non-aged. However, they failed to remedy, and in some ways even perpetuated, the existence of two highly unequal classes of the aged, both now largely dependent on direct and indirect public aid. And federal policy choices in the early 1980s tended to increase these divisions. To paraphrase a familiar quotation, our nation is moving toward two worlds of aging, one poor, one comfortable—separate and unequal.

Despite the avowed aim of restricting social welfare benefits to the "truly needy," budget policies under President Reagan in 1981 and 1982 fell far harder on means-tested programs serving the poor aged than they did on the programs most important to the middle-class elderly. Medicaid, food stamps, Title XX social services, and other heavily cut programs have been crucial to the poor aged.

This book will argue that existing old-age policies are inequitable, inefficient, and ineffective. A vast host of agencies—federal, state, local, private—with fragmented and confused lines of responsibility makes up the "aging network." Typically, the older person in need of services must deal with several sets of gatekeepers, eligibility requirements, and agency "linkages." The inherent complexity and lack of coherence of the benefit programs spawn an industry devoted specifically (though often unsuccessfully) to "case managing" and coordinating the myriad of service providers and benefit authorizers. Such a system fosters high administrative costs, long delays, and considerable inequity. When eligibility rules and programs are so complex, clients with know-how or the advice of sophisticated family members have the edge.

Our existing policies on aging tend to isolate the aged from participating in the central institutions of our society, including the family and the workplace. Rather than use their skills, we tend to "pension them off" from productive social roles, or literally remove them from society by placing them, at great cost, in institutions. Thus our system is as ineffective in meeting the emotional needs of the elderly to participate as it is in providing a reliable "social safety net" for their more concrete requirements.

Of course, if the problems of aging policy were easy, they would already have been solved. They are difficult because they involve conflicting interests and program principles. Should Social Security benefits, for example, be proportionate to contributions or to need? We currently have a hybrid whose payoff odds and consequences are understood by almost nobody outside the Social Security Administration's actuarial office—and not entirely there either. Are private pensions a matter between the employer and employee, or should they be seen as part of a national retirement-income system, with the public having an important stake in the equity and distributional results of the programs? If the costs of health care programs become prohibitive, how shall care be rationed?

Such dilemmas are difficult, but decisions must be made. In an era characterized by economist Lester Thurow as "the zero-sum society," [14] explicit choices are forced on issues which have been evaded in the past. But in order to make such choices, we need a better understanding of the aged, the impact of benefits, and the interrelationships among sources of assistance, formal and informal.

Aiding the Aged: Families and Government

Perhaps even less well understood than the role of government in assisting the aged has been the role of the family. Families are crucial for the elderly—especially those who are widowed or single. There is, however, little understanding of the extent of family help, its limitations and determinants, and expectations on both sides.

Two underlying images of the extended family's role in relation to the aged have competed in the social-scientific literature. The "isolated nuclear family" image has emphasized the structural separation between adult generations, while the "unimpaired extended family" concept has stressed the continued importance of aid between generations. The "isolated nuclear family" view is rooted in the work of classical thinkers in the social sciences who focused on the negative effects of modernizing forces on small-scale social organization such as the family. Some social scientists have argued that the structurally "isolated" nuclear family is not only a fact of our society, but a desirable adaptation to contemporary circumstances. Talcott Parsons, for example, asserted that the nuclear family is the only natural living unit in our society, and suggested that the care of the sick was a function poorly suited to the contemporary family.[15]

The "unimpaired extended" image of the family was articulated in the 1950s and 1960s in reaction to the earlier view, especially by the emerging group of specialists in aging. Many social gerontologists interpreted their research as showing that the extended family had not lost functions vis-à-vis the aged.

11

However, the evidence they cited often concentrated on sociability—visiting, exchange of telephone calls, and the like—rather than the more concrete forms of help. With regard to such activities as financial help to an aged parent, sharing a home, or personal care of impaired elders, it appears that the extended family role has, in fact, undergone significant change, and that to some extent there has indeed been a shift from family to government responsibility as benefits to the aged have grown (see chapter 3).

The actual and potential role of the family in providing for basic needs of the elderly, under contemporary social conditions, has been considerably oversold. Significant financial help from families to the aged has become a rarity. Sharing a home with aged parents or family members has been, for some years, something that both generations have preferred to avoid. With improved incomes, better availability of housing, and other social changes, the last two decades have seen a sharp decline in sharing and the concomitant availability of personal care help when needed. To some extent, assistance by government and other institutions has reduced reliance on these informal systems, and the family role has adapted to the change. Often, even the social and psychological needs of the elderly cannot be met by their children and their children's families, although strong feelings of concern and obligation are likely to exist.

Social gerontology in the eighties and beyond will need to pay more attention to the dynamics of social change. It will need to move beyond the theoretical polarities of the past, and to look critically and empirically at the role of the elderly in larger economic and social systems. It will need to be more realistic about the competing demands on the families of old people and the limitations of their ability to meet all the elderly's needs. It will need to attend more closely to the importance and value of peer relationships.

New paradigms are also needed in the analysis and development of public policies for the aging. Much more attention must be given to the actual outcomes of policies, their interaction with informal social structures, their unanticipated consequences, and their distributional effects. The majority of income for the majority of the aged comes from government checks; we spend many billions (as most people agree is proper) in maintaining the living standard of the middle class into old age. But we have not provided an adequate minimum to the oldest, the sickest, and the poorest.

Under budgetary stress, we are already seeing pressures for a return to more concrete assistance by adult children and other relatives of the aged. For example, to save Medicaid costs, the federal budget proposal for fiscal year 1983 envisioned a $180 million savings by permitting and encouraging states to charge children for the nursing-home bills of their parents. But, as we will see, it would be difficult to move far in this direction—it's hard to unscramble an omelet. The dependence on government benefits, even as they become increasingly difficult to pay for, is one aspect of the aging dilemma.

The evolution of formal benefits for the aged has been influenced by, and in turn has influenced, a myriad of other social changes. The elderly now depend on, and will continue to depend on, government or other formal programs for their sustenance. This is particularly true for income, especially for those who earned the least during their working lives and are unlikely to have saved substantial assets or to have earned a private pension. It is true of costs for acute medical care, which will continue to increase disproportionately as technological sophistication in medicine increases. It is increasingly true, too, in the important area of chronic health care. Under present-day conditions, especially with increasing numbers of married women in their middle years joining the work force, caring for a severely impaired parent can be an extraordinarily difficult and stressful undertaking for a family.

Myths of Aging

One barrier to better understanding of the real issues has been the pervasiveness of myths of old age—especially impressions of the elderly as typically decrepit and poverty-stricken. The persistence of such myths can be explained in part by their functions in validating the existing distribution of benefits and in mustering support for more of the same. The attribution to all older people of characteristics of the most deprived reinforces sentiment for across-the-board benefits to old people as a class. A sharper focus on the great differences in the needs and resources of the elderly, by contrast, would be less comfortable, since it would bring this status quo into question.

In part, too, the emphasis on the disabilities of age results from a simpler process, the natural tendency for the most troublesome, most dramatic aspect of a phenomenon to receive much more attention than the mundane. It is quite striking that the majority of elderly who are doing well are so invisible. Most people seem to think that other people's parents are, by and large, worse off than their own. The average aged person himself believes he is doing much better than most of his peers.

These myths, held to a surprising extent even by the most sophisticated, take several forms.

The myth that extreme poverty is typical of most aged. There are, indeed, many elderly who live on the edge of economic survival—too many. But grinding poverty is far from being universal or even typical. Most of the elderly poor have been poor most of their lives. Retirement can be accompanied by a significant decline in earnings, but the middle-class elderly usually can maintain a middle-class standard of living. There is a close correlation between preretirement and postretirement socioeconomic status.[16]

It is assumed even by the sophisticated that the rate of poverty among the elderly is two to three times as great as among the rest of the population. In fact, in 1980 15.7 percent of the elderly as compared to 13.0 percent of the total population had money income below the poverty line.[17]

A 1974 Harris survey found that 62 percent of the public thought "not having enough money to live on" was a very serious problem for most people over 65. Of respondents in that age range, however, only 15 percent said inadequate income was a very serious problem to them personally.[18] In 1981 the perception that severe poverty is typical of most elderly was even more strongly fixed in the public mind, despite impressive progress in the financial condition of the aged during the intervening period (see chapter 2). A follow-up Harris survey in that year asked the same question as in 1974. The proportion believing income insufficiency a very serious problem for most aged had increased, to 65 percent.[19] Only 5 percent believed that it was not at least a "somewhat serious" problem for most. But only 17 percent of the elderly felt that inadequate income was a very serious problem for them personally. The majority—58 percent—chose the "hardly a problem at all" response.

Furthermore, in a change from 1974, a majority of the public in 1981 felt that things had been getting worse for the elderly. By 54 to 38, respondents felt that older people were worse off financially in 1981 than the elderly were ten or twenty years earlier. In fact, the opposite is true—economic progress for the aged during both the sixties and seventies had been very substantial.

In 1973 the aged, who made up 10.4 percent of the population, received 11.2 percent of total national personal income before taxes.[20] Counting taxation and transfer payments, they received 13.7 percent in 1972.[21] Both subjective and objective indicators of financial distress show that the elderly with serious financial problems are a minority—an important minority, but a minority nonetheless. Respondents under 65 in the 1981 Harris survey were more likely than the aged to report that they "really can't make ends meet," and to say that "not having enough income to live on" was a very serious problem to them personally.

While there are some significant methodological problems with the Harris findings on perception of financial and other needs, it seems clear that poverty among the aged has been exaggerated. This exaggeration actually tends to move us away from a solution, by making the goal of equity seem unattainable and by diverting us from the targeted actions, directed towards those most in need, which are needed to establish an adequate floor under the economic well-being of the elderly.

Most indicators of objective financial status show that old people do have lower incomes than those in their working years, but only modestly so (see chapter 2). The lower prevalence of self-perceived financial distress among the aged may be due in part to lowered expectations, but they often really do have lower demands on their incomes. For example, 66 percent of all elderly and 70 percent of white elderly own a house that is fully paid for, as compared with fewer than half of persons aged 55–64 and 12 percent of those under 55.[22] The elderly do not, in general, have to worry about paying for children's college expenses, one of the greatest financial drains for younger families. And, since Social Security is nontaxable, and additional tax deductions are available to the elderly, their tax bills are often considerably less than those of younger families with no higher a standard of living. The elderly are actually less likely to use up savings to live on than are those under 65.[23] Altogether, the major problem with income for the elderly is not in its average but in its distribution.

The myth that physical and mental disability is typical of the aged. A small telephone survey in New York found an average public estimate that 20 percent of those 65 and older are in nursing homes. Estimates by university professors and graduate students averaged not much lower. In fact, only about 6 percent of the elderly live in institutional care settings of some kind. Perhaps an equal number are comparably disabled but are cared for by spouses, other family members, or hired helpers, or simply struggle along (see chapter 4). The vast majority of the elderly, however, are fully able to get around, to take care of themselves and often others, and to be productive. With improving health standards, fewer physically debilitating manual jobs, better nutrition, and longer life spans, the "young-old" retiree between 65 and 74 is likely to be as capable of being productive as someone in his late fifties or early sixties was two generations ago. And yet, paradoxically, fewer and fewer of those over 65 and even those in their early sixties are participating in the work force.

In the 1974 Harris survey, 51 percent of the public felt that poor health was a "very serious problem" for "most people over 65"; but only 21 percent of the elderly said that poor health was a very serious problem for them personally. In 1981, 47 percent of the public under 65 and 40 percent of the elderly felt it was a very serious problem for most elderly, while again 21 percent of the elderly found it a very serious problem for them personally.

The public also overestimates the difficulty most elderly have in securing medical help. In 1981, 45 percent of the public under 65 believed that "not enough medical care" was a very serious problem for most elderly. In fact, it is only a small group of the elderly who have difficulty securing or paying for enough medical care: 9 percent of the Harris respondents found this a very serious problem for them personally. The problems of this group are very real and important, but it's important to realize that they represent a minority.

The isolation of the elderly is similarly exaggerated in public perceptions. In 1981, 65 percent of those under 65 believed that loneliness was a very serious problem for most old people, while only 13 percent of the aged found this very severe for them personally.

The myth that the elderly are financially dependent on their children. In the New York telephone survey mentioned above, estimates of the proportion of aged receiving income from their children averaged 30 percent. The actual facts are startling—and clear. Depending on how the question is asked, it turns out that 1 percent or fewer of the elderly receive their principal financial support from children or other relatives, and that only about 4 or 5 percent at the most receive any help which is regular enough to be considered income (see chapter 3).* The elderly are twice as likely to report *providing* financial help to children as to report *receiving* it![24]

The myth that withdrawal from active social life is natural and normal for the aged. While the misconceptions listed above can be classed as popular myths, this one has been a gerontological myth. In its most explicit form, it constituted the so-called "disengagement theory" of Cumming and Henry.[25] While mostly disavowed by gerontologists today, the "disengagement" notion is nevertheless implicit in much of current aging policy and practice. For example, it is evident in our expectations about retirement and our overuse of institutions such as nursing homes. Increasingly, we retire people with many potentially productive years to the social sidelines, to a "postproductive," postresponsibility stage of life. We seem to expect the aged to feel as King Lear did (to his later regret):

> 'tis our fast intent
> To shake all cares and business from our age;
> Conferring them on younger strengths, while we
> Unburthen'd crawl toward death.
> —act 1, scene 1

The myth that the extended family system plays a central and unchanged role in the support of the elderly. This too is something of a

---

* Burdens of financial responsibility on children are a bit lighter than in the days of the prophet Elisha, who performed a miracle on behalf of a woman who cried, "My husband is dead . . . and the creditor is come to take unto him my two sons to be bondmen." 2 Kings 4:1.

gerontological myth. Many social scientists, in reacting to the earlier "isolated nuclear family" view, overreached the facts in their assertions that extended family help continues unimpaired.

The suggestion that there has been some real change is not intended to imply that there was a past "golden age" in which the generations lived together in mutual harmony. Starting with the Greek inscription that supposedly claimed that society was "going to pot" since the young no longer respected their elders, there have been myths of such past intergenerational utopias. They did not exist. The image of an American past in which most people lived in households of three or four generations has been demolished by the work of recent historians who have shown that such homes were *not* the norm, either in colonial times or later.[26] Other studies have shown the same for the European past. In fact, given the relatively small number of people who lived to an advanced age before this century, such families could not have been widespread even if the desire for intergenerational living were universal. The nuclear family was typical, in large part, simply because the elderly were relatively small in number and had many children. Up to even the relatively recent past, however, for the substantially smaller proportion of elderly in the population, more concrete help was received from families than is now provided, particularly in the form of personal care for the sick or impaired elderly.

Unrealistic or sentimental views of the strength of private social resources could have unfortunate effects. The assumption that public benefits for the needy aged merely supplement or displace family help can easily be used to justify cutting back the programs that constitute the floor under economic well-being and access to care for the aged. It is important that we look carefully and realistically at both the resources and limitations of the informal support system.

Liberal preferences for informal social structures can be co-opted by interests whose primary concern is minimizing social welfare costs. This is just what happened with deinstitutionalization in mental health. Large state hospitals were closed, without the development of community-based alternatives, in the hope that the community would somehow sufficiently provide for most of the needs of the former patients. It didn't happen. Similarly, if we are to move away from reliance on the nursing home, we will have to spend money to provide the alternatives.

When I told one acquaintance I was writing about social policy for the aged, his comment was, "I didn't think there was any." In some ways, perhaps he was right. Current programs and policies for the aging are a patchwork, reflecting incoherence, inequity, inefficiency, and a seeming lack of grounding in the facts of aging. The starting point for improving on this is a better understanding of the realities of the situation.

Old-age policy affects and is affected by forces of social and economic change. Interventions designed to ameliorate social problems have, themselves, unanticipated effects on those problems. To replace myths with facts, we need to appreciate these complex and interacting social change processes and the interplay between formal and informal structures.

In this book, we will look first at the demographic changes which are transforming our society and creating new policy dilemmas. We will investigate the family's contemporary role in caring for the elderly, and the changes in relationships between the generations that have taken place in recent years. With this as a backdrop, we can then look in detail at the two main areas in which public policy is challenged: care of the infirm aged and pension policies. This is followed by an overall look at the growth of benefits for the elderly, and an examination of who really wins in the game of aging policy. Finally, we'll discuss some of the critical public policy choices before us, and suggest some directions which could help us to make more effective, fairer use of the resources we are putting in to benefits for the aged.

Demographic developments are a particularly important underlying force in the dynamics of change. The next chapter looks at the important changes of the recent past and those to be expected in decades to come.

2

Generations of Elders

WE TEND to think of "the aged" as an identifiable, discrete group of people. But just as one can never step into the same river twice, "old age" is a status occupied by a constantly changing membership. In studying demographic change in relation to the elderly, it is useful to think in terms of the succession of cohorts, those people born within particular spans of time. Each cohort, as it reaches its later years, has experienced a unique series of historical circumstances, encountering wars, depressions, boom years, and other events at specific points in its members' life courses.

The cohort whole is greater than the sum of its parts: the experience of the individual member of a generation is affected by the characteristics of the cohort as a whole. An important example of this is the effect of differences in the size and fertility of successive cohorts. Historical circumstances influence the number of children born, on average, to the members of each cohort, and thus the size of the next generation. These fertility swings create sharp swings in the size of successive cohorts reaching old age—demographers call this "disordered cohort flow." The size and fertility of an individual's cohort are important factors in the social and economic environment he experiences over his life span.

Demography Is Destiny

Today's elderly, 25 million strong, constitute 11 percent of the population. Apart from being 65 or over, they differ widely among themselves in most important respects. As a group, they also differ in important ways both from the generations of elderly that preceded them and those which will follow.

Born, mostly, before World War I, today's elderly were often members of large families. They were young adults during the Depression, the time of the first of two major "baby busts" of this century, and had, on average, much smaller families than their parents. Among women born between 1866 and 1875—parents of today's elderly—87 percent of those who married had children, an average of 4.35 each. Among women born between 1906 and 1915 who married— today's elderly and the parents of today's middle-aged—about 81 percent had children, and these had an average of fewer than three.[1]

This means that today's elderly have on the average significantly fewer children available as a possible source of aid than did past cohorts. In 1960 elderly women who had ever been married had an average of 3.22 children; by 1970, the average was down to 2.80. The trend toward smaller family sizes for the elderly continued during the 1970s; the next group to reach old age, those who were 60 to 64 in 1970, had an average of 2.38

TABLE 2-1
Fertility by Birth Years

Years of Birth	Average Number of Children per Woman Ever Married
1866–1875	4.4
1911–1915	2.9
1931–1935	3.4
1945–1954	1.8 (approximately)

SOURCES: Mary Jo Bane, *Here to Stay: American Families in the Twentieth Century* (New York: Basic Books, 1976), appendix, table A-1; Beth Soldo, *America's Elderly in the 1980s, Population Bulletin,* 35, No. 4 (Washington, D.C.: Population Reference Bureau, 1980), p. 10.

children.[2] The baby bust of the Depression was followed by the well-known postwar boom and the equally well-known bust which began in the sixties and has continued to the present (see table 2-1). To a considerable degree, those events determined the prospects for the aged and those who must aid them, well into the next century.

The high-fertility women born in the 1920s and the early 1930s are the mothers of the postwar baby boom generation. That large generation moves through the age structure from decade to decade like the bulge in the stomach of a python that has swallowed a rabbit. The baby boom children themselves are having fewer children than any generation in history—unless there is a surprising turnaround, their fertility rate will be lower than replacement level. The only reason this has not actually produced zero population growth is because this generation of childbearing age is itself so large.

The age structure of the future population depends on whether birth rates recover from their present subreplacement levels. The very near future is the crucial time in shaping the population structure of the next century. The large postwar co-

24

hort is now in its childbearing years, and each year that passes tells us more about whether childbearing for this large group is being postponed or forgone altogether. Increasingly, it appears that the subreplacement pattern which began in the mid-sixties is being maintained.

Projected increases in the percentage of old people in the population are relatively modest for the rest of this century. If fertility remains at the present subreplacement level, we can expect the group 65 and older to go from the current 11 percent of the population to about 13 percent.[3] At replacement levels, there would scarcely be any growth in the percentage over 65. After the turn of the century, however, there will be more dramatic changes in population structure as the postwar cohort begins to enter old age (see appendix, table 1). The elderly will constitute about 18 percent of the population by 2030 if fertility increases to replacement level, and 22 percent if it remains at the present level. Even the 18 percent figure, and especially 22 percent, would have overwhelming effects on benefit systems. Given current retirement practices, there would be only about two people actually employed to pay for the support of each retiree. There would be severe pressures not only on Social Security, with total payroll tax rates in the neighborhood of 25 to 30 percent, but on other pension systems as well.

The postwar baby boom generation seems destined, as it ages, to strain institutions of the society recurringly. As children, its members overcrowded grade schools, creating a child-centered society in the 1950s. During the 1960s, universities were crowded, and the "youth culture" flowered. In the 1970s, competition became tight for advancement in corporations, for tenure on university faculties, for jobs in good law firms, for promotion to welfare supervisor and police sergeant. It seems likely that in the next century this cohort will be crowding the nation's nursing homes. In fact, assuming no change in the use of nursing homes within age groups, the

Health Care Financing Administration[4] projects a 132 percent increase in nursing home populations by 2030.

Changing Circumstances, Changing Needs

Today's elderly differ from their predecessors (and from those to come) in more respects than just numbers. Until about 1950, roughly half the elderly were men. Today, women live substantially longer than men. As recently as 1960, there were 83 elderly men per 100 elderly women, but in 1979 there were only 68 men per 100 women.[5]

Women usually marry men older than themselves, and now live an average of eight years longer. The result is extended widowhood with little opportunity for remarriage for large numbers of elderly women. A woman widowed at 65 can expect to live for an average of sixteen years more.[6] Among those 75 and older in 1978, 70 percent of the women and only 24 percent of the men were widowed. Among those 65 to 74, 41 percent of the women and 9 percent of the men were widowed.[7]

Severe need in old age has now become and will continue to be largely a woman's problem. The widowed and the very old are the most likely to be unable to meet their basic physical, social, and personal care needs, and women predominate in both these groups. There are two women 85 or older for each man of this age; among the widowed elderly (65 and older), four out of five are women. Yet retirement income systems, especially private pensions, serve men much better than women, as shown in chapter 5. Poverty is becoming feminized among the aged as well as (for somewhat different reasons) among those of working age.

Another important and relatively recent change has been a shift in living arrangements among the elderly. As recently as

1960, 60 percent of widowed women 75 and older, and 50 percent of those 65 to 74, lived with relatives. By 1980, that proportion had dropped to only 33 percent of those over 75 and to 27 percent of those 65–74. Indeed, the current generation of elderly is the first for whom living alone has become the norm when a spouse is not in the picture.

Retirement is not usually thought of as a recent invention. The current generation is the first, however, for whom retirement by 65 could really be said to be the rule, and the first for whom retirement before that age was at all common. As recently as 1950, almost half of elderly men were in the work force, while this is the case for only one-fifth of the current generation (see appendix, table 3). And the Bureau of the Census has projected a further decline, to less than 17 percent, by 1990.[8]

The men in the current generation of elderly are retiring, on average, substantially earlier and living longer, so the period of retirement is being lengthened at both ends. Many now retire well before they are officially "elderly." Between 1955 and 1975, the proportion of men aged 60 to 64 who were no longer in the work force doubled to 34 percent; it was projected to reach 37 percent by 1980 and 43 percent by 1990. And unlike earlier generations, where substantial numbers continued to work even after 70 (28 percent of men as recently as 1955), only 13 percent of men 70 and older were projected to be in the labor force in 1980, and 10 percent in 1990.[9]

Along with the more extended "postwork" stage, the typical life course now includes a much longer "empty nest" postparental stage. In 1940 the period between the marriage of the last child and death was about 17 years for white women. By 1960, a woman's average age at the time of the marriage of her last child had gone down by three years while life expectancy was up by seven years.[10] Thus the postparental stage was lengthened by 10 years. By 1980, with the addition of about three more years to life expectancy[11] and with the number of children being smaller, the period lengthened further, reaching almost twice its 1940 average.

Thus we are experiencing something that, on a mass scale, is new in human history: a long period of time in the typical life course beyond the stages of work and family responsibilities. Looked at from one point of view, this development represents a great historical accomplishment: the chance for everyone to be a gentleperson of leisure, if only for one stage of life. The troubles in this Paradise stem from the slowness of institutions to adapt to the changed needs of the newly supernumerary; from the absence of the satisfactions of being productive and useful; and from the uneven distribution of resources with which to enjoy leisure. Most important, however, while economic and demographic developments of the last several decades favored the emergence of the "postresponsibility stage," the circumstances of the coming decades will make it hard to continue this way.

Changing Resources

The trend to earlier retirement can probably be largely attributed to the increased income entitlements created by public and private pension plans. Time-series analyses seem to suggest a causal relationship between increases in Social Security pensions and lowered retirement age.[12] Pension improvements caused the incomes of the aged relative to those of the rest of the population to increase rapidly during the sixties and seventies, even though they earned less and less from work.

Commonly accepted images of the elderly assume that severe and unrelieved poverty is typical, even increasing. Such portrayals are made even by extremely knowledgeable observers. For example, according to a Pulitzer Prize winning 1975 book by a renowned gerontologist:

Changing Resources

Two crucial and distressing facts about poverty and old age are clear. First, although the numbers of those in poverty in other age groups are said to be decreasing, there has been an increase in both the number and proportion of aged poor. . . .in 1969 there were approximately 4.8 million people aged 65 and older who were living in poverty, almost 200,000 more than in 1968. In this same period. . . poverty declined by 1.2 million for all other age groups.

Second, the elderly are the fastest-growing poverty group. . .[13]

In fact, during the 1960s and the early and mid-1970s, both the proportion of the elderly who were below the poverty level and the actual numbers of poor elderly declined. During the early seventies, especially, the rate of poverty among the aged dropped substantially while poverty among the non-aged remained stable. Throughout the sixties, the rate of poverty among the aged was double that of the non-aged, while today the aged are only slightly more likely to be in poverty (table 2-2).*

Other estimates, which take into account in-kind income not considered in the official poverty definition, suggest that the improvement has been even greater than table 2-2 indicates.[14] It should be noted, however, that 26 percent of the elderly in 1980 were within 125 percent of the poverty level, versus 18 percent of all persons. As with poverty, near-poverty was concentrated among the usual suspects: women, nonwhites, and those not living in families. A majority of black elderly—53 percent—were in poverty or near-poverty.[15]

The general improvement came almost entirely from unearned income provided by income transfers and pension programs. The elderly are distinctive among major social groups in the degree to which their economic well-being depends on government programs. Half the income going to old people comes from government transfer payments,[16] and, as we will describe further, much of the rest comes from private pensions

* The 1968 to 1969 increase in poverty among the aged was accurately stated, but it was a minor fluctuation, statistically insignificant in the Census Bureau's sample.

TABLE 2-2

Number and Percent of Persons in Poverty

	Persons 65+		All Persons	
Year	Number (000's)	Percent	Number (000's)	(Percent)
1959	5,481	35.2	39,490	22.4
1967	5,388	29.5	27,769	14.2
1968	4,632	25.0	25,389	12.8
1969	4,787	25.3	24,147	12.1
1970	4,709	24.5	25,420	12.6
1971	4,273	21.6	25,559	12.5
1972	3,738	18.6	24,460	11.9
1973	3,354	16.3	22,973	11.1
1974	3,308	15.7	24,260	11.6
1975	3,317	15.3	25,877	12.3
1976	3,313	15.0	24,975	11.8
1977	3,177	14.1	24,720	11.6
1978	3,233	14.0	24,497	11.4
1979	3,586	15.1	25,345	11.6
1980	3,871	15.7	29,272	13.0
1981	3,853	15.3	31,822	14.0

SOURCES: U.S. Bureau of the Census, "Money Income and Poverty Status of Families and Persons in the United States: 1976, Advance Report," *Current Population Reports,* Series P-60, No. 107, 1977; "Social and Economic Characteristics of the Older Population: 1978," *Current Population Reports,* Series P-23, No. 85, 1979; "Money Income and Poverty Status of Families and Persons in the United States: 1980, Advance Data from the March 1981 Current Population Survey," *Current Population Reports,* Series P-60, No. 127, 1981. Personal communication, Bureau of the Census, 1982.

and is subsidized by "tax expenditures." Despite the general improvement and the increased reliance on public programs, the distribution of income among the elderly population remains highly skewed, with the bottom group getting a small share not only of total income but of government benefits. The wide gap between the median and mean incomes of the elderly, indicative of this highly skewed distribution, has not diminished while the proportion of the elderly's sustenance coming from government has increased. The distribution of assets is even more highly skewed.

Changing Resources

The decline in poverty among the aged would have been even more dramatic were it not for the increased percentage of the elderly living alone, who now account for three-fifths of the elderly poor. In 1959, 58 percent of the poor elderly lived in families, while in 1976 only 36 percent did so. The elderly not in families were 2.3 times as likely as those in families to be poor in 1959, 3.9 times as likely to be poor in 1975.[17] As table 2-3 shows, between 1959 and 1975 the proportion of elderly in the living arrangements most at risk of destitution increased; but the effect of this was far outweighed by the improvement within each living arrangement.

The decline in poverty was not evenly distributed. It was relatively greater for men than for women, for those in families than for those living alone, and for whites than for nonwhites. Thus, the poorest categories of elderly improved less than the better-off categories (see appendix tables 4 and 5). Between 1959 and 1971, both elderly whites and blacks made progress in coming out of poverty; but from 1971 to 1980, black elderly made virtually no progress. Their poverty rate decreased only from 39.3 to 38.1 percent, while the rate for whites went from 19.9 to 13.6 percent (appendix, table 4). In 1959, black elderly were a little less than twice as likely as whites to be in poverty; by 1980 they were almost three times as likely.

TABLE 2-3
Poverty Rates by Living Arrangements, 1959 and 1975

| | | In Families | | | | |
Year	All Persons	Head	Wife	Other Member	Total	Alone or with Nonrelatives
1959:						
% in Poverty	35.2	29.1	30.5	17.4	26.9	61.9
% of Elderly in Living Arrangement	100	39.4	20.0	16.6	76.1	23.8
1975:						
% in Poverty	15.3	8.9	8.2	4.3	8.0	31.0
% of Elderly in Living Arrangement	100	37.7	21.1	9.4	68.7	31.6

SOURCE: U.S. Bureau of the Census, "Characteristics of the Population Below the Poverty Level: 1975," *Current Population Reports,* Series P-60, No. 106, 1977.

There has been a change in the pattern of need to which assistance programs have not yet responded. Today hard-core need (and living at the poverty level represents spartan living indeed) is concentrated heavily in a double- triple-, or quadruple-jeopardy group—without spouse, living alone, female, minority, or all of these. Yet we still tend to perceive the problem as it existed fifteen or twenty years ago, when hard-core need was much more widespread, and the effort was to remedy the condition of the aged as a whole. The focus now needs to be shifted from economic improvement for the elderly generally to the equitable distribution of benefits and the needs of those left behind in the general improvement.

The number of elderly with high incomes increased substantially in recent years, producing a skewed income distribution with mean income considerably higher than the median. In 1980, mean and median were $16,918 and $12,881 respectively for elderly-headed families, $7,176 and $5,095 for individuals outside families.[18] Adjusting for family size and for the known underreporting of Social Security income in official income statistics, it has been estimated that mean per-capita income of households headed by elderly persons is exactly equal to per-capita income of households headed by the non-elderly.[19] If in-kind aid is added, the elderly have a higher mean per-capita income than the non-elderly. Median per-capita incomes, however, lag those of the non-aged by 18 percent.

Trends in mean income, as with poverty rates, have favored the elderly in recent years more than the non-elderly. With indexing of benefits, their incomes survived stagflation better than those of workers. From 1972 to 1977, real (inflation-adjusted) mean incomes of all families and unrelated individuals declined slightly while mean real incomes of the aged increased by about half a percentage point annually. Between 1979 and 1980, mean real incomes of the non-elderly dropped by 5.5 percent while real mean income of the aged did not change significantly.[20]

Other Changes

The relative growth of the elderly population and the changes in the economic situation of the aged are probably the most important developments for public policy. But they are by no means the only important changes.

In recent years, the elderly have differed considerably from the rest of the population in their level of education. Recent cohorts of elderly had grown up in times when a long period of schooling was not nearly so widespread as it is today. The resulting difference in the education of the old and the young contributed to a "generation gap" often perceived as a function of age per se. In 1970, the difference was at its greatest, with a median education of 12.2 years for the population 25 and over and 8.7 years for those 65 and over. Typical educational attainment of the elderly was only 71 percent of that of the total adult public, down from 81 percent in 1952.[21]

This gap is already beginning to close again as a better-educated generation reaches old age. The elderly of 1980 have a full year of education, on average, more than those of 1970, and educational levels will continue to converge as generations affected by the rapid growth in formal education of the 1920s, 1930s, and 1940s come to predominate among the elderly. By 1990, we will have an elderly generation with a median education just about at the high school level (11.9 years), bringing them up to more than 90 percent of the average for all adults.[22] This will be a considerably more sophisticated generation, with much capacity for organized economic, social, or political activity. The replacement of a generation with many foreign-born members by a predominantly American-born generation should also help to narrow the "generation gap."

To the surprise of many experts, life expectancies at later ages, relatively stable between 1954 and 1968 after previous growth, are again on the rise. For men, life expectancy at age 65 increased by half a year between 1969–71 and 1974, after remaining constant for the previous fifteen years. For women, the increases were even greater. Female life expectancy at 65 is now almost eighteen years, as compared with less than fifteen at midcentury.[23] These changes, together with the decline in fertility, have made obsolete earlier projections of the proportion of elderly in the future population.

Indeed, the possibility that future medical developments could produce an abrupt and therefore unexpected change should not be entirely discounted, as demographers tend to do. Two scenarios are possible. In the "one-horse shay" version, the length of healthy old age will increase. In another less attractive scenario, medical technology will keep increasing the numbers of "worn out" elderly who are kept alive for long periods in a helpless state and at great cost. Sophisticated and costly life-support systems, organ implants, diagnostic equipment, drugs, and surgical treatments may create increasingly difficult ethical and policy dilemmas. When an artificial heart becomes feasible, will we pay to install one in each older person whose own heart wears out? Will we instead allow only the wealthy elderly to have them, and retreat from the ideal of a one-class system of care? Such problems could make issues like kidney dialysis, which has newly emerged as a multi-billion-dollar Medicare-financed industry, seem small.

However, the period of healthy old age in the future may be longer than we now assume. Health statisticians are currently puzzling over a somewhat unexpected decline in the death rate from strokes (37 percent lower) and from heart attacks (25 percent lower), over the past decade in the United States. The potential effects of progress in these areas on the duration of old age are greater than those of progress in other areas of medicine. Thus, elimination of the major cardiovascular-renal diseases (principally heart diseases and stroke) would produce an increase in life expectancy at age 65 of 11.4 years, while the elimination of cancer would increase life expectancy of the elderly by only 1.4 years.[24] Progress in cardiovascular medicine

Other Changes

appears to be responsible for a significant part of the recent improvement in life expectancy at age 65.

These causes of death are also strongly linked to life style and are responsive to preventive medicine. Smoking, high-fat diets, overweight, and insufficient exercise are strongly correlated with cardiovascular disease. Survey data show a marked jump in the proportion of non-elderly Americans who exercise regularly; this change in habits has not yet affected those who are now elderly, but there is hope that if these changes do not turn out to be only a fad, they may pay off in the future in a healthier and longer-living elderly generation.* Preventive medicine could have important effects on future mortality rates of the aged—for example, in more consistent application of simple existing treatments for asymptomatic hypertension, which is a leading factor in the deterioration of kidney, heart, circulatory and brain function by the time old age is reached. Emphysema, bronchitis, and other lung conditions largely caused by smoking are major disabling diseases of old age. It has been recently shown that consistent exercise can substantially prevent the development of osteoporosis (weakening of the bones), the cause of the "broken-hip syndrome" which so often results in institutionalization. And exercise has a preventive effect on osteoarthritis, another of the major cripplers.

Our health budgets are increasingly dominated by the enormous costs of treating the diseases of the elderly in hospitals and caring for their infirmities in nursing homes. These efforts have had measurable payoff in reducing morbidity and even mortality, but to a considerable degree the investment in acute care has reached a point of diminishing returns. Health care of

* Though I look old, yet I am strong and lusty;
  For in my youth I never did apply
  Hot and rebellious liquors in my blood,
  Nor did not with unbashful forehead woo
  The means of weakness and debility:
  Therefore my age is as a lusty winter,
  Frosty, but kindly.
          —Shakespeare, *As You Like It*, act 2, scene 3

35

the elderly in our system is episodic, fragmented, and lacks a preventive focus. The return on investment in preventive medicine and health education for the future health of the elderly may be much greater than the marginal payback from acute care expenditures. As it stands, Medicare through cost-plus reimbursement offers almost a blank check to hospitals, while programs to improve the nutrition of the aged and other programs which contribute to prevention have been heavily cut.

Respiratory cancers are a major and increasing cause of disability and death among the aged,[25] while many other forms of cancer are decreasing. They are responsible for more than 100, 000 deaths per year, with the death rates highest by far among the elderly. Eighty percent or more of these deaths are caused by smoking, as well as much cardiovascular disease and other conditions. Smokers have a 70 percent higher death rate from all causes than non-smokers;[26] altogether, it has been estimated that tobacco is responsible for 320,000 premature deaths per year, and for 10 million sufferers of debilitating chronic diseases at any given time.[27] It has been projected that an 8-cent a pack increase in cigarette excise taxes, which the Reagan administration considered and then dropped in early 1982, would have ultimately reduced the number of young men who start smoking by 15 percent,[28] and would also reduce smoking (by a lesser percentage) among current smokers. The direct health care costs of cigarette smoking were estimated for 1976 at $8 billion per year, and indirect costs at $19 billion.[29] Surveys have shown that a substantial proportion of the public still is not aware of well-established medical findings about the effects of smoking. Public policies designed to have a serious impact on the rate of cigarette smoking—through such measures as high taxation, educational programs, more specific health warnings—could have a significant effect on the future health of the elderly.

Medical progress (and, conceivably, changes in lifestyles)

could result in an even larger elderly population by the next century than present projections provide for. Further increases in medical sophistication are also likely to increase the cost of medical care, of which the elderly are the chief consumers. As the cost per unit of medical care provided (such as a day of hospitalization) increases, and the number of units consumed rises, the expense of medical care will become an even more central political and social issue.

When Is a Person "Old"?

The conventional yardstick of age 65 as the threshold of "old age" is arbitrary. As the first head of the Social Security Administration put it, "We more or less picked it out of a hat." Nevertheless, it has become enshrined in our laws, in our statistics, and, ultimately, in our thinking.

Age 65 now represents an earlier point in the life cycle than it did when Social Security was enacted. One proposed alternative definition of "old age" is the age at which life expectancy is an additional ten years.[30] On this basis, the threshold of old age was 69.1 in 1930, 72.5 in 1960, and 73.7 in 1970. Paradoxically, recent generations have attained physical old age later and later while reaching social old age, the transition to "retired" status, earlier and earlier.

The focus on the conventional age-65 criterion can be misleading in understanding demographic developments. At any given time, the population aged 65 and older consists of several cohorts of varying size. The proportion of the population 65 and over will actually level off during the remainder of this century. But more significant for human services needs, the "old" will be older than they are now as the large cohort born in the early years of this century reaches its late seventies and eighties. The "frail" population 75 and over is expected to increase by 53 percent by 2000, and the population 85 and older by 64 percent.

As we have seen, the current generation of elderly differs markedly from previous and future generations. During the coming years, we can expect even greater variations in the resources and needs of the aged than before. This will make policies which implicitly assume uniformity of needs even less appropriate than before.

There will be a "young-old" group, with many personal and economic resources, beginning a retirement phase increasingly close to the prime of life. But there will be another group likely to be left behind in the general but uneven spread of pension and age-specific benefits. The trend to independence which works well for the comfortably-off couple in their sixties, who can travel and enjoy life, will work less well for the 80-year-old widow living on Supplemental Security Income and in failing health, whose single child left home thirty years ago and lives half a continent away. The issue will be whether we can afford to finance the early retirement of the former and still provide for the needs of the latter, for whom the informal support system promises little concrete help.

3

The Family
Support System

THE FAMILY plays a vital but widely misunderstood role in meeting the needs of the elderly. Family and government interact in complex ways, and their roles have changed substantially in recent decades.

Research on the facts of family help to the aged has been more limited than the issue deserves. Analysts who stress the strengths of the extended family in providing help have often tended to concentrate their attention on the extent of sociable contacts such as visiting and telephone calls, rather than concrete assistance. Much has been made of data showing that most elderly live within easy visiting distance of at least one child, but not enough is known about such important matters as how families respond to health crises of elderly parents.

While important, sociable interactions can go just so far in meeting the elderly's needs. The trend toward greater independence in concrete aspects of life, such as living arrangements and finances, has important implications. While at any given time most of the population over 65 is physically and mentally able, sooner or later each older person will probably face a period of incapacity. When that happens the principal resources are formally organized programs (still largely nursing homes) and the family, especially family in the older person's household; paid helpers play a relatively small part. Thus the growing independence in living arrangements among the elderly has a direct bearing on the need for publicly provided chronic care.

Living Arrangements

In 1980, 41 percent of women over 65, and 15 percent of men over 65, lived alone. The difference does not result from divergent preferences, but from the fact that women are much more likely to be widowed (51 percent of the women as compared with 14 percent of the men). The living arrangements of widowed women are much like those of widowed men, those of never-married women like those of never-married men.[1]

Increasingly, widowhood means coping not only with the loss of the spouse but with living alone. Among widows 75 and over, at greatest risk of impairment, the proportion living with children or other relatives dropped during the 1960s and 1970s by 1.5 percentage points per year—from three-fifths in 1960 to one-third in 1980. The rate also dropped by nearly half for the younger elderly (see appendix, table 2). The living arrangements of the elderly in 1980 are shown in table 3-1.

The family offers almost the sole alternative to solitary or institutional living. While friends are important to the aged, they only infrequently share living arrangements.

In true old age especially (after age 75) men and women face very different situations. With the decline in intergenerational households, the presence of a spouse is the main alternative to

40

Living Arrangements

TABLE 3-1

Living Arrangements of the Elderly in Households, 1980

	65–74		75+	
	Men	*Women*	*Men*	*Women*
Married, Living with Spouse	79.4	48.1	67.7	22.1
Living with Relatives but without Spouse	6.5	14.5	9.3	26.0
Living Alone	11.6	35.5	20.9	49.3
Living in Home of Nonrelatives	1.6	1.1	1.4	1.2
Living in Own Home, with Nonrelatives	.9	.8	.7	1.4
with one adult man	.2	.4	.1	.5
with one adult woman	.6	.3	.6	.7
all others	.1	.1	—	.2

SOURCE: Calculated from U.S. Bureau of the Census, "Marital Status and Living Arrangements: March 1980," *Current Population Reports,* Series P-20, No. 365, 1981.

living alone; but at that stage in life a spouse is present for only one-fifth of the women, as compared with two-thirds of the men. Of 7 million elderly Americans who live alone, just under 80 percent are women. Being alone (like being poor) in old age is for the most part a woman's problem.*

Sharing living quarters across generational lines—elderly parent with adult child—has declined much more rapidly than among family members of the same generation. During the past two decades, the shift away from family living arrangements was much greater among the widowed than among those of the elderly who had never married.

In 1960, elderly widowed women were more likely than those who never married to live in families, because they could and did move in with their children when their husbands died. By 1979–80, however, they were considerably *less* likely to live in families, largely because of the decline in shared living quarters between older people and their grown children. The same trend can be seen in the case of men.

* And almost 70 percent of the residents of nursing homes are women; see chapter 4.

TABLE 3-2
Percentage Living in Families
Among Widowed and Never-Married
Women in Households, 1960 and 1979–80

	65–74		75+	
Year	Single	Widowed	Single	Widowed
1960	51.5	50.2	52.4	59.9
1979–80	38.3	27.0	37.5	33.3
Change	13.2	23.2	14.9	26.6

SOURCES: Calculated from U.S. Bureau of the Census, *Census of Population: 1960, Persons by Family Characteristics,* Subject Reports, Final Report PC(2)-4B, 1964; "Marital Status and Living Arrangements: March 1979," *Current Population Reports,* Series P-20, No. 349, 1980; and "Marital Status and Living Arrangements: March 1980." Data from 1979 and 1980 are averaged to increase the sample size and reliability.

For old men, widowhood, now typically leading to living alone, is particularly stressful. Men are more liable to let their living conditions deteriorate, since they have been less habituated to caring for a home. They have fewer peers in similar circumstances, since more of their contemporaries and friends are likely still to be married. Often the wife had taken the lead in maintaining kin ties. Some studies have found that widowhood is followed by death more often for men than for women. It should be remembered, however, that old men have a much better chance to remarry, and those who remain unmarried may be atypical and have more psychological difficulties to begin with than widows.

The decline of coresidence has real consequences for the availability of help when the elderly become disabled. Once separate living arrangements have been established, it becomes increasingly difficult for families to rearrange themselves to provide care for an impaired older person. Today, shared households are often those in which the adult child never left home, rather than being formed by the elderly parent moving in with the child. Census figures show that increasingly, in intergenerational households, the elderly person is reported as the head of the household. Among widowed women 65 to 74 living in families, 60 percent were heads of household in 1980 as against 41 percent in 1960.[2]

In the past, middle-aged married women were available to take in elderly parents and care for them. But these women are now much more likely to be in the labor force, and thus unable to provide such care. Labor force participation by married women increased from 20 to over 44 percent between 1947 and 1975.[3]

Sharing with nonrelatives did not fill any of the vacuum created by the shift away from family living. Instead, it has also declined. One once-important subset, lodging arrangements, accounted for about 5 percent of widows 75 and older in 1950 but only about 1.5 percent in 1970.[4]

How can we explain these changes in living arrangements? They do not result simply from changed attitudes about sharing versus living independently, as some sociologists have suggested.[5] Public opinion data do not in fact show growing disapproval of shared housing between the elderly and their grown children: in fact, the reverse has been true.

It is more reasonable to conclude instead that these trends result largely from economic changes and public policies, especially the expansion of pension systems. With increased economic independence, the elderly have been able to act on long-standing preferences for independent living. Living with children, and particularly living in a home headed by one's child, has often been associated with economic dependence. With the elderly enjoying greater financial independence, these are the arrangements that have declined.

Income-maintenance policies have also created an incentive for living alone. In the Supplemental Security Income program, the basic means-tested income benefit for the elderly, a recipient's grant is substantially reduced if he or she lives in the home of a relative.

The Effects of Fertility Trends

Another factor should not be ignored: fertility differences between generations affect the odds that an older person will live with family. The first prerequisite to living with children, or receiving care from them, is having had them at all; as we shall see, the more children one has the more likely he or she is to live with one of them in old age.

Thus, part of the change of the last two decades can be explained by the fact that today's elderly are of a generation that had fewer children than their earlier cohorts. The central experience of their young adulthood was the Depression, a time when marriage was postponed and childbearing was often given up entirely. Woody Guthrie sang of the dustbowl:

> The sweethearts sat in the dark and they sparked,
> They sat and they kissed in that dusty old dark,
> They sighed and they cried and they hugged and they kissed,
> But instead of marriage, they talked like this—
>
> So long, it's been good to know you,
> But I've got to be drifting along.
>
> —Woody Guthrie, SO LONG, It's Been Good
> To Know Ya (Dusty Old Dust), © 1940, ren.
> 1968. Courtesy Folkways Music Publish-
> ers, Inc.

We examined the shifts in the fertility patterns in the previous chapter, focusing on aggregate (cohort) characteristics. But turning to the individual level of analysis, what effects do these family structure differences have on the living arrangements of particular elderly persons? The coincidence of aggregate changes in fertility and aggregate changes in living arrangements tells us little by itself about causation. What we need to know is whether elderly individuals with more children are actually less likely to live alone. Table 3-3 shows that this is precisely what happens.

TABLE 3-3

Living Arrangements by Number of
Children Ever Born to Widows 65+, 1970

	Percent in Specified Living Arrangement			
Number of Children	In Families	In Non-Family Households	In Institutions, Group Quarters	Total
0	18.7	71.7	9.6	1020
1	32.4	58.0	9.6	1029
2	36.0	55.8	8.2	1164
3	40.6	50.8	8.7	867
4	38.7	53.0	8.3	651
5	46.7	47.1	6.2	403
6	51.0	43.8	5.2	306
7+	57.3	38.1	4.6	634

SOURCE: Analysis of Public Use Sample data from the 1970 United States Census, 1:1000 sample.

Those elderly with the most children are almost twice as likely to live in families as those with only one child. And the probability of being institutionalized is less than half as great for those with the largest families as for those with the smallest. Fertility changes account for only a small proportion of the changes in living arrangements and institutionalization, but they do contribute to current pressures on the system of aging benefits and to the trend toward independent living. It can be estimated that a difference in family size of one child increases the odds of living in a family for elderly widows by about 3 percentage points.[6] Thus, about a tenth of the change in living arrangements from 1960 to 1970 can be accounted for by the trend in fertility.[7]

Attitudes toward Sharing a Home

Public opinion is divided on the desirability of coresidence. One question in national surveys asked: "As you know, many older people share a home with their grown children. Do you

TABLE 3-4

Coresidence Approval by Age
and Marital Status, 1973–78
Percent Responding "Good Idea"

Marital Status	18–39	40+
Single	51.9 (699)	38.6 (145)
Ever-Married	35.8 (2,072)	27.2 (2,967)

think this is generally a good idea or a bad idea?" In 1978 and 1980, negative responses to this question somewhat exceeded positive ones.[8]

The survey responses distinctly fail to support several stereotypes about this issue. For example, respondents living in a large city did not show a more removed attitude toward the extended family. On the contrary, they were the most likely to consider coresidence a good idea. These differences persisted even when race was controlled for. Working-class and less educated respondents were less, not more, "extended-family oriented" in their responses. Nonwhites were the most supportive of coresidence. The elderly themselves were most strongly opposed (see appendix, table 6).

The most important factors determining attitudes on coresidence, however, were what one might call "lifestage" factors: age and marital status in particular. It seems that the closer one comes to actually encountering the situation, and the greater are the conflicting pulls of a new nuclear family, the less one approves of coresidence. Both age and marriage had negative, independent effects on approval of coresidence (see table 3-4). Young single people approve of coresidence; but when they have formed new families of their own, those ties compete with their sense of filial responsibility.

Marriage represents a rite of transition, after which the relationship between child and parent is expected to change.* The

---

* "Therefore shall a man leave his father and his mother, and he shall cleave unto his wife. . . ." (Gen. 2:24).

new nuclear family becomes the primary focus of responsibility and day to day sharing.[9] The multigenerational family lacks clearly defined cultural roles. As a result, expectations can clash; in our cultural setting, the elderly as well as their children may feel that "no kitchen is big enough for two women." The sharing of a home tends to create conflict between the culturally assigned roles of the original family and the new family —conflict, for example, between the role of son and that of husband. Innumerable mother-in-law jokes attest to the institutional strain between these roles.[10]

Is it true, as has been argued,[11] that "the large increase in the proportion of widows living alone results from a change in family norms governing living arrangements of the elderly"? An analysis of change over time in attitudes on shared living does not support this proposition. This analysis made use of archival data from a 1957 survey, generously made available by the National Opinion Research Center (NORC), and data from the replication in NORC's General Social Surveys of 1973, 1975, 1976, and 1978 discussed above. It showed a steady decrease in disapproval of the idea of coresidence and an increase in approval.[12] For this trend analysis, respondents 18 through 20 in 1973–1978 were excluded to match the 21 and over range of the 1957 survey (see table 3-5).

Clearly, the change in living arrangements is not the result of change in attitudes. What we must look at are more concrete

TABLE 3-5

*Coresidence Approval, 1957 to
1978, among Respondents 21+*

Year	Good Idea	Depends	Bad Idea	Total Respondents
1957	28.2	8.3	63.5	2567
1973	30.4	11.5	58.1	1433
1975	29.9	15.9	54.3	1399
1976	35.4	15.2	49.4	1411
1978	34.1	17.0	48.9	1459

changes in circumstances, especially those created by social policies such as improved pensions. The question then remains: Why have attitudes toward sharing become more positive as sharing itself declined? Perhaps it is precisely because fewer old people live with their children today. Since it is no longer the only alternative, the truly difficult home situations may be less common.

Today's elderly, and most 1957 respondents, lived through the Depression when there was much doubling up as a matter of sheer economic necessity.[13] Sharing a home under these conditions or under other pressures[14] may have been more difficult than it would be today. There may also be an increasing tendency on the part of the public to see the problems of the elderly as revolving around isolation rather than simple deprivation,[15] although there is evidence that economic deprivation for most aged is still assumed.

A cohort analysis tells us more about where the change in coresidence attitudes is coming from. It is not simply a matter of individuals changing their minds. On average, members of the generations who were over 40 in 1957 actually became somewhat more negative about coresidence. But older generations were replaced by a younger generation much more favorably disposed to coresidence; and the cohorts who were under 40 in 1957 became more favorable (see appendix, table 7).

What effect, if any, these more "communal" attitudes among the younger groups may have, and whether these opinions will change as they age, is at present unknown. However, since the change has been concentrated among those least likely to be involved in a shared home, any effects on behavior may be limited.

Choices in Need

In open-ended telephone interviews conducted for sociologists Lee Rainwater and Mary Jo Bane in 1979,[16] people were asked if they would ever want to move in with their children. Objections centered on two themes: the need for independence and privacy on the part of both generations, and the fear of being a burden.

Never; we get alone fine, but there's no house big enough for a multiple family.

I wouldn't want to do it; my children will have their own lives . . . My grandfather lived with my family and it caused a lot of problems. I wouldn't want to go through that again.

I never will; I'll move into a pup tent before I'll move in with them.

Never—I'm a homosexual and it would put a strain on them to have me there with them.

Under *no* circumstances would I go with any of my children.

A minority of those responding thought the idea was acceptable, but were not particularly enthusiastic.

As long as I wasn't in the way, it would be O.K.

I think children should take care of their parents . . . *Would you share a home with children?* If I was disabled or something like that, and couldn't take care of myself. Or too old. *How would you feel about that?* I don't know, it would depend on their attitude. I only know about the other end. I feel my parents would never be a burden to me. I hope my children will feel that way about me.

The optimum level of closeness, for some respondents, was somewhere between the usual alternatives of living alone and living in a child's home.

I would only if we could be completely separated. I mean if we could have a separate apartment in their house ... As long as the parents can maintain their own separate rooms, then it is fine. The children are close enough in case help is needed and you can enjoy each other's company, but then you can leave so they can have their own privacy.

Interviewees often saw the consequences of impairment as a choice between moving in with relatives and moving into a nursing home. This was generally seen as a choice between the frying pan and the fire. A man who responded, "I'd never do it—period!," to the question on sharing a home with children answered the nursing home question with, "Heavens, no! I'd rather die first! I like my independence and no one will ever put me away."

True, some respondents had faith in the concern of their children:

Move to nursing home? Do not intend to! I hope not! I came over from Europe and it's different over there. Nursing homes are for old sick people with no family to care for them.

Move in with kids? Only if I had no choice or if it was that or a nursing home.

Nursing home? I suppose if we—couldn't take care of ourselves, but our kids wouldn't let that happen. I have five children ... they'd never let us go into a nursing home.

Even so, some seemed to feel a nursing home would be preferable to dependence on children or relatives.

Well, I'd move in [to a nursing home] before I'd be a burden to someone. I've lived my life and I don't want someone to have to give up their time to take care of me. I wouldn't want to but I would before I'd be a burden on my relatives. [However] I don't approve of nursing homes. I've had some experience with them and even the best ones are bad.

Financial Help

Share with children? Never! My mother went into a home—she wanted to be by herself and so do I—I don't want to be a burden to anyone.

Most often, respondents said these were matters they had not thought about and preferred not to—since none of the solutions were good. The impact on families which do take on such care is in fact profound. It often creates a collision between obligations to parents and to spouse and children. A heavy load of guilt is likely no matter what choices are made[17] (see chapter 4). Consequently, even respondents whose parents were in their late eighties seemed to have given the matter little thought. One such man simply said, "Fortunately, their health is holding up." When disability happens, plans have often not been made.

Financial Help

In the past, especially in hard times, families were an important source of income for the elderly. In 1937, it was estimated that 45 percent of the aged were dependent for income on friends and relatives. A total of 35 percent were self-supporting—28 percent through wages, savings, and investments, and the rest through private or public employee pensions. Eighteen percent depended on federal income maintenance programs, and only one-tenth of 1 percent were sustained by grants from private charities, with about 2 percent supported in public or private institutions.[18]

Similarly, in 1940, two-thirds of Americans over 65 reportedly were receiving some kind of family or other aid.[19] A 1944 study estimated that 30 to 40 percent of aged parents were supported by their children. Two-thirds of the respondents agreed that "we should look to children to support aged parents."[20]

It is widely believed that financial help given by children to aged parents still plays a major role. In the 1960s, some sociologists suggested this was becoming increasingly significant as a source of financial support for the aged.[21] The notion that the family continues to have major potential for the financial support of the aged also plays a part in the recurring suggestion that public pension programs need not constitute an adequate retirement income by themselves. It is assumed that savings and family contributions will supplement these programs. However, those on the lower rungs of the socioeconomic ladder can seldom accumulate sufficient savings to play a major role in retirement income, while family contributions now play a very small role for almost all elderly.

The fact of the matter is that financial help from families has just about disappeared as a significant source of income for the elderly. Its decline dates back at least to the 1950s. Today it is virtually a negligible component of the elderly's income.

According to 1976 census data,[22] only 1 percent of the elderly reported receiving any income from personal contributions, family or otherwise. Income from personal contributions was trivial among virtually every demographic subgroup. Even among nonmarried elderly women and among aged blacks, the estimate was only 1 percent.

Compare the income sources reported for 1976 with those mentioned earlier for 1937. Employment has declined; in 1976 only 19 percent of the aged had any income at all from wages or salaries. The big difference, however, is in receipt of pensions. Eighty-nine percent of the elderly sample had income in 1976 from Social Security. In addition (usually in combination) 20 percent had income from private pensions or annuities, 9 percent from government employee pensions; 6 percent had veterans' pension benefits. Only 11 percent had any income from need-tested public assistance programs, including Supplemental Security Income.

The 1981 Harris survey of the aged inquired about sources of income to the elderly person's household. Only 5 percent of elderly reported that any income came from "parents, children, or other relatives."[23]

The 1974 Harris survey asked about family financial help in more detail. One question, phrased in a different way than in 1981, asked older people to list the sources of their own income. Only 4 percent included "children or other relatives." Questions about in-kind assistance in the form of food, clothes, or rent also elicited very few positive responses. Financial help from children or other relatives was the largest source of income for fewer than 1 percent.[24]

Another question asked whether children or grandchildren "ever help you in any of the following ways," listing various forms of assistance including "help out with money." About one-fifth of the elderly said that they ever received such help; for most, apparently, it was not regular enough to be considered "income." Almost four-fifths, however, still said "no." Only when the question was asked in this way were there even sufficient positive responses for a detailed analysis of the receipt of help.

The balance of aid was not from the adult children to the elderly parents, but vice versa. Among white elderly, fewer than 20 percent reported receiving financial help from children, while 46 percent said they provided such help to their children. (Detailed results of the analysis of financial help patterns are provided in the appendix, tables 8–11).

Receiving financial help, even in this limited form, was largely a correlate of poverty among the elderly. Even though lower income elderly are likely to have lower income children, help with money was largely confined to this group (see appendix, table 10). Thirty-three percent of elderly with income under $4,000, as compared with 13 percent of those with income over $7,000, received help from children. Black elderly were two and a half times more likely than whites to receive financial help—half the black elderly and one-fifth of the whites did so (appendix, table 8). Unlike the whites, the black elderly were as likely to get help as to give it.

The greater financial help between generations of blacks, like their more frequent sharing of a home and lower use of institutional care, suggests patterns of greater interdependence between generations which benefit the aged. Children respond to the more severe economic need of their parents who, in turn, are more likely to be useful and needed in child rearing and maintaining the home. These patterns suggest that the image of a "tangle of pathology," with a resulting shift from family responsibility to government dependency, does not apply to the extended family ties of the black elderly. Extended family adaptations to nuclear family instability and poverty seem to have some useful results for the minority aged, making family help more available to them.

The difference by race in rates of family financial help is confirmed by results from two other studies. In a survey of inner-city elderly,[25] mostly quite poor, 33 percent of black elderly and 20 percent of white elderly received financial help from children. Analysis by the author of data from the Michigan Panel Study of Income Dynamics found that among elderly women in 1975, 7.8 percent of blacks and 3.0 percent of whites reported receiving "income" from relatives.[26]

With increasing income, older people are more likely to provide help to their children and less likely to receive it. The ratio of giving to receiving was 4 to 1 for higher-income elderly. Even the lowest income elderly, however, were more likely to give financial help than to receive it (appendix, table 10). Receipt of help is also concentrated among the elderly with only a grade-school education—27 percent of these were helped versus 11 percent of the college-educated. More than a quarter of blue-collar and of farm elderly were recipients, versus fewer than an eighth of white-collar respondents (appendix, table 11). As one might expect, too, it is primarily the widowed elderly who are helped. But even they gave more often than they got, by their own report.

Most of the elderly who report receiving help are those who are living with children, particularly those living in a home headed by a child or other relative. Half of this group received family help.

These data suggest strongly that family financial help to the elderly is not the norm. Even those who receive help appear somewhat uncomfortable about it. Only 19 percent of those who actually were receiving financial help from their children seemed to think children *should* play this role.[27]

Number of children is also a predictor of family financial help. As we found with living arrangements and with institutionalization, smaller family sizes mean lower probabilities for help being available. Financial help was received by 14.6 percent of those with one child and 19.8 percent of those with two, as compared with 36.2 percent of those with five or more. This means that the trend to smaller family sizes has had a downward effect on frequency of family financial help to the aged.

Since financial help is simultaneously affected by a number of factors which are themselves intercorrelated, the causal relationships are somewhat complex. The joint effect of several of these variables can be assessed by causal modeling techniques (path analysis). A model of the effects of race, sex, marital status, and income on the receipt of financial help from children indicates that race, marital status, and income all affect financial help significantly, and independently of one another. Men are considerably less likely than women to receive help, but this difference disappears when their higher income and greater chance of being currently married is controlled for. The racial differences survive controls for income and marital status.[28]

As we've seen, when it does exist, family financial help to the elderly is usually not regular or substantial enough to be considered "income." Clearly, the family can no longer be counted on to fill the gaps in income programs.

Attitudes toward Financial Help

Do these patterns of actual behavior accord with expectations—those of the elderly or those of their children—as to a child's proper role? We know that children still feel a strong sense of obligation and concern for their elderly parents, that existing income support programs are perceived as inadequate, and that widespread financial deprivation is assumed. We know, too, that support for coresidence has increased even while coresidence itself has declined. Given this, we might expect that the public would continue to think family financial help to the aged appropriate and desirable.

Actually, financial help to the elderly seems no longer to be perceived by the public as a family responsibility. Belief that children should be a source of income to the elderly when they are no longer working was distinctly a minority position in 1974. Only 10 percent of the public included children among the sources which should provide such income. Filial aid was thought appropriate least often by the elderly themselves (7 percent) and most often by those under 40 (13 percent).

Normative support for filial aid is greatest among those with the most education, and among white-collar and farm respondents. Interestingly, black respondents were *less* likely to support aid (only 6 percent) although they actually provide more of it. The married elderly are especially unlikely to think of their children as potential income sources. Urban respondents support filial aid more strongly than those in suburbs and towns, but less strongly than rural people (see appendix, table 12, for detailed findings on financial help attitudes).[29]

Attitudes toward Financial Help

TABLE 3-6

Sources Considered Responsible by Public
for Income Support of Elderly in Retirement
Percent Specifying Source

Source	1957	1974
Self	27.5	33.8
Children	52.5	10.3
Pension (private)	16.1	45.5
Government (non-specific)	33.3	27.6
Social Security	41.6	67.3

SOURCES: Analysis by the author of survey data on financial help attitudes. Baseline: Shanas/NORC 1957 Health of Older People Study. 1974 data: Harris/NCOA Survey of the Aged. Multiple responses were permitted.

Financial help attitudes have changed dramatically since the 1950s. Expectations for help from children have been displaced by expectations from formal help systems—private pensions and Social Security (see table 3.6).

Within cohorts, individuals on average dramatically changed their attitudes about intergenerational financial help between 1957 and 1974 (see appendix, table 13). Apparently, the change in attitudes followed the change in actual behavior, which had taken place earlier as pension systems provided for basic income needs of most elderly. The prediction[30] that the trend in financial help attitudes was away from the norm of financial independence and toward financial help to the aged which would "increasingly help in the latter's retirement" did not turn out to be the case.

Why did normative support for financial help decline while normative support for coresidence increased? Clearly, these items do not tap the same dimension of "extended family orientation" in the sense of a unitary underlying disposition that either increased or decreased. Rather, government and private responsibilities in various areas of life are being redefined. The public seems to believe (contrary to the facts) that severe financial privation of the elderly is more typical now than ever. But it no longer sees the family as the responsible party.

If Social Security and private pensions do not fill the bill, it is unlikely that the family will come back out of the woodwork to provide for the aged. If anything, it is remarkable how frequently even low-income elderly find satisfaction—and, perhaps, a nurturing role they are familiar and comfortable with—in continuing to help their children financially. The strong feeling that the aged should *not* have to depend on children financially is one clue to the powerful emotional support for Social Security and opposition to cuts, which the Reagan Administration discovered to its chagrin. This support is apparently not seriously impaired by an equally strong impression of financial unsoundness and administrative waste in the program (see chapter 5).

Apparently, the public sees bureaucratically organized programs as capable of handling, and now responsible for, income needs of the elderly, but not necessarily nonfinancial needs. People seem more inclined to look at the family as a resource for care of the impaired aged. The increasing support for co-residence which has developed among younger people may be tapping attitudes about this; it may also reflect a growing dislike of nursing homes.

Life Satisfaction and Family Interaction

Emphasizing the importance of family relationships, many gerontologists have given less weight to friendships. One classic review of the literature on aging, for example, describes ties with friends and neighbors as "less important to older people than children and other relatives, serving more as a complement than substitute for kinship association."[31]

Life Satisfaction and Family Interaction

As we have seen, however, the family role in meeting concrete needs is less than is often assumed. Even for the psychological needs of the aging, family ties are often less satisfying than is supposed. Some studies have found that people who see their children less have higher morale than other older people.[32] Another study found no relationship between frequency of contact with children and morale, but found that peer contacts could make an important difference in morale.[33] Using a larger and more representative sample than these, and holding constant factors like income, health, marital status, age, and race, analyzing the 1974 Harris data for elderly respondents with children by multiple regression shows that both frequency of contact with children and whether the respondent lived with children had only very small, though significant, effects on scores on a life satisfaction scale. Living with children had a small negative effect while seeing children had a small positive effect. Number of friends, however, had a much larger effect, in the positive direction.[34]

As discussed in more detail below, there are also indications that the elderly, particularly those who have lost spouses, employment relationships, and other ties, have higher morale when their housing circumstances encourage convenient, informal interaction with friends and neighbors—for example, when they live in age-concentrated housing. Participants in peer networks which tend to emerge naturally in age-dense housing help one another in a number of important ways, and can more easily develop new relationships and participate in community life. The implications of this for public policy are considerable.

Cross-National Variations in Extended Family Roles

Does generational independence inevitably follow economic modernization? On the whole, Western European patterns are similar to those in the United States. In several Western European and Scandinavian countries, however, patterns seem more "nuclear" than those here.

In the Netherlands, for example, about 12 percent of the elderly live in old age and nursing homes.[35] Only about 5 to 10 percent live with children or grandchildren.[36] More than 80 percent of the Dutch in homes for the aged were reported to be receiving general-assistance support from local authorities. Dutch attitudes toward family financial support appear to be at least as negative as in the United States. In one survey, only 8 percent of old people considered children responsible for the elderly's financial support.[37]

In Scandinavian countries, there are up to twice the number of institutional beds per capita as in the United States. (U.S. states in the upper midwest with large populations of Scandinavian origin and cold climates, such as Minnesota, also have bed supplies that far exceed the U.S. average). In England, on the other hand, nursing homes have been used less than in the United States.[38] All these comparisons are difficult, however, because of the greater extent of home care programs in Europe.

In the less modernized countries of Eastern Europe, extended family patterns appear more prevalent. In Poland, for example, it has been estimated that 67 percent of old people with children live with them.[39] It is unclear to what extent this is a result of the housing shortage. When asked whether the family or society should help an elderly person when in need, the overwhelming majority of Poles chose "society." In Yugoslavia, nearly 70 percent of old people with children live with them.[40] Countries like these with high rates of coresidence also tend to have low rates of institutionalization of the elderly.

Overall, there is a rough correspondence between extended family patterns and level of development. Japan, however, is an important exception: despite economic development, it still has a strong extended family system. In 1973, 74 percent of all Japanese 60 and over were living with grown children. Sixty-one percent lived with married children, compared with 4 percent in Denmark, 8 percent in the U.S., and 12 percent in Britain. Living alone for the aged has been rare in Japan until relatively recently,[41] though it is apparently increasing.

In the early 1970s, only 1.3 percent of Japanese elderly were in institutions. Financial help from children to parents appears to be common, both within and between households. Seventy percent of Japanese aged 60–69 believe "it is natural to live together" or that it is better to live together when possible. Elderly parents appear to perform useful functions within the family.[42]

What have been the implications for government? Whether the greater family role is the cause, the result, or some of both, government aid for the aged has been slower to develop in Japan than in the United States and Western Europe. For each person 65 or older, the Japanese government spent $174 annually in 1964–67 on social security and welfare, compared with $942 for the United States. The next lowest spending level among industrialized nations was found in France with $432 annually.[43] The growth of pension systems in Japan has been slower and considerably more limited than in Western industrialized countries. Only 7 percent of the elderly qualified for significant pensions in 1970, the rest having access only to more limited benefits providing little more than "pocket money."

Japan, of course, has followed a different path to development than the United States and Western Europe. Many aspects of economic modernization are quite recent despite the high standard of living which has been reached. (The effects of scarce and costly housing supply must also be kept in mind.) It is not yet clear what changes will follow economic development, over time. However, Japan is not immune from the processes taking place elsewhere in the industrialized world, which are increasing demand for and costs of benefits for the aged.

In the early 1970s, the problems of the elderly, or *rojin*, became a focus of public attention in Japan, and benefits were considerably expanded in what the Japanese, with their penchant for borrowing English words, called the *rojin buumu* or old-people boom. Pension benefits were increased by a factor of more than five between 1969 and 1975, and indexed to wages and the consumer price index. Free medical care for those over 70 was implemented, senior-citizen centers were built all over the country, and over 30 new programs for the aged were initiated.[44] All together, social welfare spending, of which the elderly are the most conspicuous beneficiaries, increased from 5.8 percent of GNP in 1970 to 10.6 percent in 1976, and to an estimated 13 percent in 1980. At the same time, the percentage of elderly living with children has apparently declined to some extent. According to one 1982 estimate, it has dropped to 46 percent nationwide, and to 40 percent in Tokyo.[45] Concern about burdening children has apparently become more widespread among Japanese elderly, and American-style retirement communities have even begun to sprout up.

In addition to family support, two other aspects of the Japanese system have reduced reliance on pension systems. One has been Japanese agricultural policy. At considerable cost in crop subsidies, as well as in agricultural inefficiency and the resulting extra food imports, Japan has sought to maintain small family plots, many of which are country homesteads for city dwellers. The elderly often "retire" to tending these small plots.

Japan has also maintained high employment of the elderly, apparently without negative effects on innovation or economic dynamism. There is mandatory "retirement" at 55, but in most cases retirement seems to mean a new job in another company, another job in the same company, a position in a subsidiary—often arranged by the original employer—or self-employment. For instance, the elderly are encouraged to operate small urban stores. A majority of men over 65 in Japan are still working, as compared with about one-fifth in the United States.[46] This probably is motivated by economic need, given the still relatively limited pension system.

The Japanese case represents one end of the spectrum among modernized economies. Even there, the direction of trends is the same as elsewhere. Demographic shifts much like those expected in the United States, but occurring at an even faster rate, will result in dramatic social changes in the next several decades.[47] Japanese policymakers worry about the implications of projections that 18 percent of the population will be over 65 by the year 2000—up from only 8 percent in 1950—for Japanese innovation, lifetime employment systems, expectations of continued though slow promotion through seniority, and other traditions. Virtually all the advanced industrial world, in fact, is experiencing such changes in demographic structure, leading to a slow-growing population dominated by the aged and to increasing cost burdens for their benefits.

Potentials and Limits of the Family Support System

Fashions in interpreting the extended family's relationship to the aged have gone through wide pendulum swings. "Functionalist" social thinkers of the 1940s and 1950s focused on the negative effects of modern conditions on extended family functioning, and made too little of the very real importance of family in the elderly's lives. Partly in overreaction to this, and partly in response to new empirical evidence of the family's continued importance to the elderly, many of the emerging community of social gerontologists in the sixties and seventies characterized the extended family as playing an unimpaired and unchanged role in meeting the various needs of the aged.

Distinctions were not fully made among the different aspects of extended family interaction: between sociability and concrete help, for example.

In fact, the extended family's role *has* been changed in important ways. Relying increasingly on benefits provided or subsidized by government, the elderly came to depend less on help from relatives or their own current economic efforts. This shift, by and large, meets with public approval: respondents in the 1981 Harris survey were more in favor of increased government responsibility for the aged than of increased reponsibility by their children.[48]

Up until the 1950s, the question of family financial responsibility for the elderly was a persistent problem in social policy, notably in the administration of the Old Age Assistance program. In many states, the authorities struggled with very limited success to enforce relatives'-responsibility laws.[49] These rules may have had some effect in controlling public assistance costs in some states—more from deterring applicants than from actually eliciting family contributions for welfare recipients—but they were almost impossible to enforce in an equitable fashion. It was seldom practical to force a contribution from a child by process by law. The only other way to enforce the provisions was to withhold or reduce assistance if a relative were deemed able to contribute. This put welfare workers in the position of making particularistic judgments about the ability of families to pay and inevitably led to selective enforcement.

State relatives'-responsibility rules both for Old Age Assistance and for Medicaid were barred by federal legislation and regulations during the 1960s. This reflected the change in public opinion on financial help reported above, the difficulty and inequities involved in administering family contribution rules, and the trend toward more objectively verifiable, more uniform criteria in the administration of social welfare. This latter trend was capped in 1974 when the state Old Age Assistance programs were folded into the new Supplemental Security Income program, administered by the Social Security Administration. Medicaid remained with the states, with federal cost-sharing; the ban on required relatives' contributions proved important, especially in the light of the increase in the share of Medicaid going to nursing homes.[50] The Old Age Assistance experience gives little reason to expect much success from the 1982 federal proposal that the states require children of the elderly to pay part of their parents' nursing home bills. Public sentiment seems to provide little, and decreasing, support for expectations of major *financial* responsibility from children for aged parents, though there appear to be stronger expectations for in-kind help with the care of the sick aged.

As we show in chapter 4, children play an important role in caring for the sick or impaired elderly, but most of this help takes place in shared households and is provided in kind. It is remarkable how seldom this role extends to paying for care provided by someone else, either in an institution or in the parent's separate home. A 1976 study found that children contribute only about 1 or 2 percent of typical nursing home bills,[51] and the percentage of nursing home care paid by government has been increasing.

Our review indicates the very real limitations as well as the strengths of the family support system. The changes discussed in these first three chapters have fueled dramatic growth in public spending for the aged, which in turn has further fostered the growth of independence between generations and the aged's dependence on public benefits. In the following two chapters, we will look at the growing public role in two central areas: care of the chronically impaired and income maintenance policies. These two areas are at the heart of the emerging crisis in public policy for the aged.

4

Long-Term Care: Government and Family Roles

WITH retirement income systems in place, financial help is no longer widely seen as a family responsibility. In the care of the sick and impaired aged, it is less clear: family and public roles overlap. Over the last two decades, the public role has expanded greatly.

Despite expansion of publicly funded home care, nursing homes are still the major alternative when the family cannot carry the load. They house only about 5 percent of the aged, but the cost per patient is so high that they make up a $20 billion industry. More than half of this is now publicly paid.

The Growth of Nursing Home Care

The Growth of Nursing Home Care

Public expenditures for nursing home care increased almost a hundredfold between 1960 and 1979—from $108 million to over $10 billion (see table 4-1). Part of the increase can be attributed simply to the increased elderly population (the numbers over 65 increased by 21 percent in the sixties and 23 percent in the seventies). More significant has been the fact that the old are growing older. The very old, who are at much higher risk of institutionalization, have increased much faster than the total elderly population.

Fewer elderly are now in mental hospitals, and this accounts for another part of the nursing home increase. In 1960 there were 178,000 elderly in mental hospitals nationally, in 1970 there were 113,000.[1] This was part of an overall reduction in patient census that continued through the seventies: state hospitals cut their population, young and old, from 560,000 in 1955 to about 150,000 in 1981[2] (see also appendix, table 14).

But even within age groups and adjusted for the mental hospital shift, use of nursing homes has gone up. Living alone more often now, the aged are less likely to have someone on hand to help when the need arises. Today's elderly have had fewer children, reducing the odds that one will be available for their care. And the middle-aged women who traditionally cared for them are now likely to be working. Asked what would happen if her parents came to need more day-to-day care, one woman replied: "My father may—and if so, he would go to a VA hospital or nursing home . . . I work so I couldn't quit to care for them so I guess it'd be a facility of some kind."[3]

Finally, the charge per day of nursing home care has increased much faster than the general rate of inflation. In the early sixties, many nursing homes were "mom and pop" affairs, often in converted houses. Homes opened after this period were built more on the hospital model, and cost more to construct and operate. Many of the older homes, which often

67

had problems with fire safety, were closed down. In 1976, the average skilled home charged $10,900 per year,[4] and the cost is closer to $20,000 today. In some urban areas, charges are even higher; in New York City in 1982, the average was about $28, 000. Between 1973 and 1977, average per-diem rates increased 55 percent, half again as fast as the cost of living.[5]

Like the physical design of nursing homes, the ratesetting and regulatory procedures applied to them are borrowed from the hospital world. Nursing homes, however, are predominantly profitmaking while hospitals mostly are not. Cost-plus rate formulas, and understaffed inspection agencies, have left plenty of room for manipulation and outright fraud in claiming reimbursement.[6] In some states nursing homes have been sold back and forth from one entrepreneur to another at inflated rates, padding the property cost base which goes into the Medicaid rate. Even after strenuous regulatory efforts, property reimbursement represents a high part of the total rate structure. A simpler, traditional method of cheating involves claiming nonexistent or personal expenditures for reimbursement as operating costs. Even where enforcement is toughest—as in New York, with a large special nursing home prosecutor's office and strengthened laws in the wake of the mid-seventies scandals—cheating still takes place, and shady characters remain in the industry. In 1982, Bart Lawson, the head of the major association of New York nursing home operators, was indicted for allegedly paying to have a union-organizers' trailer bombed during a strike, and attempting to claim Medicaid reimbursement for the payoff.

Flat-rate reimbursement systems are no panacea, either—they encourage skimping on food, staffing, and materials, and make it even more difficult to control and monitor quality of care. Altogether, the marriage of public financing and private entrepreneurship which has typified the nursing home industry has been plagued with problems and cost inflation. The cost of monitoring adds to the total expense.

Financing Nursing Home Care

High rates quickly exhaust patients' funds, and push all but the wealthy onto Medicaid eventually. In addition, as rates increase and social attitudes change, laws prohibiting the transfer of assets from the elderly to their children or others in contemplation of establishing Medicaid eligibility become increasingly difficult to enforce.[7]

Financing Nursing Home Care: The Family and Government

Most government expenditures on nursing home care are paid out through Medicaid—nursing homes in 1978 accounted for 42 percent of total Medicaid expenditures.[8] Medicaid, unlike Medicare, is means-tested, and descends from "welfare medicine" programs for public assistance recipients. Medicaid generally requires that the patient first exhaust his own resources on the nursing home care, retaining $25 a month or so for personal items.

In 1979, Medicaid paid for 57 percent of all nursing home expenditures, Medicare accounted for 2 percent, the Veterans Administration another 2 percent, and private insurance only .7 percent. Most of the costs not covered by Medicaid were paid by the patients themselves.

Often, once assets are spent, both patient and Medicaid contribute to the cost of care, the patient "spending down" Social Security or other income while Medicaid pays the rest. Thus, while Medicaid pays for about half the total, about three-quarters of nursing home patients receive at least partial Medicaid support,[9] and the great majority of long-term patients end up on Medicaid.

Medicare, federally financed and administered without a means test, plays only a small role in nursing home care. In the initial years of Medicare, its role was more substantial, though benefits were limited to sixty days of post-hospital "extended

69

care." In 1968, the program paid $348 million in extended-care bills, but by 1972 stricter criteria for this benefit had reduced payments to $155.6 million.[10] Medicare benefits have been restricted to those patients who need physical therapy or other specialized services for rehabilitative, not maintenance, purposes; other limitations apply as well. In 1979 Medicare paid $373 million of a much larger nursing home bill; this accounted for only 2 percent of total nursing home costs and less than 2 percent of the total Medicare program.[11]

The dramatic growth of the nursing home industry, and the shares paid by public and private sources, can be seen in table 4-1. Total costs, and the cost to government, have more than doubled each five years for the last two decades. The implementation of Medicare in the late sixties caused a jump to 70 percent in the proportion which was publicly financed, falling to 42 percent in 1972 after Medicare cutbacks. The proportion rose again to about the 55 percent level in the late seventies, with Medicaid as the main source.

Between 1973 and 1979, the increase in total public and private nursing home expenditures was 148 percent, versus a 64 percent increase in the consumer price index. Nursing home care has been the fastest-growing cost in the health system, increasing in recent years in the neighborhood of 18 to 20 percent annually.

For some kinds of assistance, private welfare systems[12] play a major third role along with governmental and private expenditures. For retirement income, private pensions are important, while private insurance accounts for 75 percent of nongovernmental hospital expenditures. However, for nursing home care, the role of private welfare is insignificant, since privately bought or employee insurance accounts for less than 1 percent of the costs. The need for nursing home care is less unpredictable, more determined by social factors, than other forms of care; the problem of "adverse selection"—the disproportionate purchase of the insurance by high-risk patients—and other

Financing Nursing Home Care

TABLE 4-1
Nursing Home Costs and
Public-Private Shares, 1960–1979

Year	Costs (millions)			Percentage from Public Sources
	Public	Private	Total	
1960	108	419	526	20.5
1961	174	432	606	28.7
1962	275	420	695	39.6
1963	337	554	891	37.8
1964	406	809	1,215	33.4
1965	494	830	1,324	37.3
1966	692	835	1,526	45.3
1967	1,192	666	1,858	64.2
1968	1,466	604	2,070	70.8
1969	1,726	735	2,461	70.1
1970	1,665	1,195	2,860	58.2
1971	1,973	1,309	3,282	60.1
1972	2,465	3,395	5,860	42.1
1973	3,173	3,477	6,650	47.7
1974	3,806	3,649	7,450	51.1
1975	5,014	4,086	9,100	55.1
1976	5,856	4,744	10,600	55.2
1977	7,184	5,434	12,618	56.9
1978	8,369	6,463	15,120	55.4
1979	10,102	7,705	17,807	56.7

SOURCES: Burton D. Dunlop, *The Growth of Nursing Home Care* (Lexington, Mass.: Lexington Books, 1979); Robert Gibson and Charles R. Fisher, "National Health Expenditures, Fiscal Year 1977," *Social Security Bulletin*, 41, No. 7, 1978: 3–20; Health Care Financing Administration, *Long-Term Care: Background and Future Directions*, Discussion Paper (Washington, D.C.: 1981).

difficulties make long-term nursing home care almost uninsurable on a private basis.

Notwithstanding the extensive government participation, nursing home costs can be devastating to individuals. The impoverishment resulting from nursing home costs reduces the chances of leaving the nursing home and re-establishing life outside, even if health improves after a convalescent period; and in fact few patients who stay for more than a few weeks ever return to the community. The lack of incentive for the nursing home to help patients move out, the absence of public social services serving this function, and the complexity of re-establishing housing arrangements and needed services all contribute to the very low rate of return to community life. If arrangements were made to maintain and pay for the patient's home during a convalescent period, and if needed assistance is provided, probably more could leave the nursing home than actually do. As regulators put increasing pressure on hospitals to discharge patients once the need for acute care is passed, we will need to organize ourselves better to use nursing homes on a short-term basis as well as for "permanent placement."

The burden of long-term care is particularly difficult because of the great cost of extended stays. Even the middle-class elderly end up using Medicaid. In terms of lifetime social class affiliation, race, and other social characteristics, long-term care Medicaid clients are quite different from other Medicaid clients. Of nursing home patients for whom Medicaid was the main payment source in 1977, fewer than 10 percent were nonwhite.[13] The children of nursing home patients, who are not required to contribute, are generally not poor; children named as next of kin had a median income of $14,676 in 1976.[14] Largely because of nursing home expenses, the average elderly Medicaid recipient in 1976 used (in addition to Medicare reimbursements) almost six times the cost of services used by the average child on Medicaid under age six, and 5.4 times the cost of services used by Medicaid recipients between the ages of six and twenty. The sense that expenditures are out of control has led to severe Medicaid cuts in most states, often substantially affecting poor children and their parents. It is often not fully appreciated how much of the Medicaid growth has come from nursing home costs, not care for the younger poor. These costs account for an ever-increasing share of Medicaid.

The financial impact of nursing home placement on a spouse

remaining in the community can be very severe, particularly if the institutionalized spouse was the source of income for the household. The Health Care Financing Administration[15] has reported that this can force the noninstitutionalized spouse to enter an institution as well. A Census survey found the spouse of a nursing home resident contributed an average of $2025 in 1976, out of an average income of $7980.[16]

The frequency and amount of contributions from other family members, including children, were much less. This is consistent with our findings on income, suggesting that extended family help does not tend to involve money. Contributions toward care from children named as next of kin averaged only $160. Brothers and sisters named as next of kin provided an average of only $37 per year.

Social Factors: Race

Social factors that are strongly correlated with the use of long-term care include race, marital status, and number of children (parity). In 1976, 95 percent of residents of long-term care institutions were white (there were 970,000 whites and 56,000 nonwhites).[17] This represents approximately 28 nonwhites and 49 whites per 1000 in the community[18] (see table 4-2).

Other things equal, the poorer health of nonwhite elderly would mean more nursing home use, not less. White elderly in 1971–72 averaged 34 days of restricted activity due to illness or injury per year, while nonwhites averaged 53 days. Forty-two percent of whites and 54 percent of nonwhites were limited in activity due to chronic conditions.[19] Nonwhites do not reach nursing homes until they are more impaired than is true for whites. Of 1977 nursing home residents, blacks were more likely than whites to require assistance in dressing, toileting,

TABLE 4-2
*Utilization of Long-Term Care
by Race and Sex, 1976*

	Number of 65+ in Care	Number of 65+ in Community	Number in Care per 1,000 in Community
White	970,070	19,654,000	49
Male	299,040	8,049,000	37
Female	671,030	11,605,000	58
Nonwhite	55,610	2,008,000	28
Male	23,490	864,000	27
Female	32,120	1,144,000	28
Male	322,530	8,913,000	36
Female	703,150	12,949,000	54
Total	1,025,680	21,662,000	47

SOURCES: U.S. Bureau of Census, "1976 Survey of Institutionalized Persons," *Current Population Reports*, Special Studies, Series P-23, No. 69, 1978; "Marital Status and Living Arrangements: March 1976," Series P-20, No. 306, 1977.

walking, and eating, and more likely to be incontinent.[20] Nonwhites are less likely to be considered medically able to have remained at home with appropriate services.[21]

The family role in nursing home admission differs for whites and nonwhites. In 1976, 34 percent of whites and only 15 percent of nonwhites in long-term care learned of the facility through the next of kin. Nonwhites were much more likely to have been referred by a social agency or a court.[22] Elderly nonwhites who do end up in nursing homes may be the ones with no family at all. In 1977, 22 percent of black nursing home residents were receiving no visitors, as compared with 11 percent of whites.[23] Of long-term care residents in 1976, 17 percent of blacks versus 8 percent of whites had no family or relatives on record.[24]

Nonwhites were less likely to have been admitted by a family member, and twice as likely to have been admitted by an official source. The choice of institution was less likely to have

74

been made on the basis of such factors as convenience of visiting. Location was the reason only a third as often as for whites, 18 versus 54 percent. For nonwhites, the choice was almost three times as likely to have been made by an official or to be the only institution available.[25]

In contrast to their lower use of nursing homes, nonwhites are more likely than whites to be institutionalized in state mental hospitals.[26] Thus nonwhite elderly are more likely to have their problems attributed to mental deviance rather than old age and feebleness. Of elderly blacks in nursing homes in 1973–74, 14.3 percent had been transferred from mental hospitals, versus 7.5 percent of whites.[27] In 1976, 26 percent of nonwhite residents were officially under the guardianship of the institution, the state, or a court and in that sense were labeled as incompetent, versus 12 percent of whites.[28]

Elderly black women, in particular, underutilize nursing homes. These patterns may reflect the important position of the grandmother in black families.[29]

Utilization of long-term care institutions by blacks was only 57 percent that of whites in 1976. These differences may be due to discrimination in access to nursing homes, to cultural preferences and greater likelihood of family care among blacks, or to a combination of these factors. The result is that fewer public resources are spent per capita on black elderly for institutional long-term care.

These differences may belie, in one respect, the "tangle of pathology" view[30] which would tend to see blacks as overconsumers of public subsidies because of their impaired family structure. To some extent, the extended family plays an adaptive role in coping with the stresses encountered by black families and the nuclear family instability that ensues. Grandparents can often serve a useful purpose in maintaining a household and in helping with children; reciprocity is perhaps the best basis for a shared home. Among widowed women 75 and older in 1979, 46 percent of blacks versus 66 percent of whites lived alone; the blacks were much more likely to be in families.[31] The difference in living arrangements was even greater by race among women 65–74.

Social Factors: Marital Status and Number of Children

The crucial role of social supports in determining the use of long-term care is shown dramatically in the relationship between rates of institutionalization and marital status. The married elderly are much underrepresented in institutions, the widowed (most of whom have children) are in the middle, and the never-married are much overrepresented. Among the widowed, those with the most children have the least chance of institutionalization, as shown in chapter 3. The relationship between marital status and institutionalization is shown in table 4-3.

Marital status accounts for the greater use of nursing homes by women, at least among whites. In 1970, 3.8 percent of men 65+ and 5.7 percent of women 65+ were residents of institutions.[32] Women were at greater risk of institutionalization because they were much more likely to be widowed. Elderly women, who on the average married men older than themselves, live to more advanced ages and have fewer opportunities to remarry. Within marital status, sex differences in institutionalization rates are small.

The more children an older person has had, the smaller the odds of institutional placement. The percentage for widows was 9.6 for those with no children or one child, and only 4.3 percent among those with seven or more children (see chapter 3, table 3-3). Each additional child decreases the probability by .5 percent.[33]

It is interesting that having just one child seems to do little

Marital Status and Number of Children

TABLE 4-3

*Marital Status of Elderly in
Institutions and in the Community, 1976*

Marital Status	Residents of Long-Term Care Facilities, 65+	Residents of Households	
		65+	75+
Married	16.7	55.2	40.1
Widowed	63.6	36.7	52.4
Never married	14.6	5.3	5.6
Divorced	4.0	2.8	1.8
Not reported	1.1	—	—

SOURCES: Calculated from U.S. Bureau of the Census, "1976 Survey of Institutionalized Persons" and "Marital Status and Living Arrangements: March 1976."

to guarantee family care. Not all children are equally available as caretakers. Daughters are much more likely to take on this role than sons; often, one or more children in a family will move far away; some children have their own family responsibilities that compete with parental obligations. A particularly likely caretaker is the child who never married and never moved out of the parental home; in large families, it is much more likely there will be such a child.

The finding that use of institutions does vary with family size, and the fact that the current elderly have had smaller families than those of one or two decades ago, suggest that fertility changes have contributed to the increased use of nursing homes. The current generation of young adults is having even fewer children, and this may contribute further to high demand early in the next century.

It is difficult to quantify the contribution of the various factors we have discussed on present and future nursing home demand and utilization, not to mention their interaction, but some approximations can be made. Based on our data on the effects of number of children, it can be estimated that perhaps 10 to 15 percent of the increase in the proportion of the aged in nursing homes between 1960 and 1970 (from 2.3 to 4.0 percent) can be attributed to smaller families.[34] Around a quarter of the change could be attributed to the shifting of mental hospital patients to nursing homes (see appendix, table 15). Another 20 percent of the growth can be attributed to the change in age structure within the population 65 and older, with increasing percentages in the oldest groups.[35] It appears that something over half of the increase can be attributed to these three developments. The rest is the result of the expansion of coverage and cost-related rates for nursing homes under Medicare and Medicaid, which made the field more attractive to enter and thus expanded supply; the improved pensions that increased the rate of living alone among the elderly; the reduced number of nonworking women available as caretakers; and other factors.

Formal and Informal Care

Families, not nursing homes, still provide the majority of care to the mentally and/or physically impaired elderly. For every resident of a nursing home, it can be estimated that there are between one and two similarly impaired individuals living in the community;[36] a reasonable middle ground estimate is 1.5. The General Accounting Office[37] estimated that 10 percent of the total elderly population could be classed as "extremely impaired." Of this group, 37 percent were in institutions while the rest were in the community, representing 7 percent of the non-institutionalized elderly. About 75 percent of residents of institutions fell into the "extremely impaired" class. Another 8 percent of the residents of institutions fell into the "greatly impaired" class, but only 8 percent of all those who were "greatly impaired" were in institutions.

Based on data from the large National Health Survey, it has

been estimated that in 1977 there were 1.6 million noninstitutionalized persons who were impaired in their ability to independently carry out such basic activities of daily living (ADL) as bathing, dressing, eating, and going to the toilet, most of whom were elderly, as compared with 1.2 of the 1.3 million total in nursing homes and similar institutions with such limitation.[38]

By this estimate, 35 percent of those 85 and over were dependent in ADL, and 61 percent of these were in nursing homes. Eleven percent of those 75–84 were dependent, of whom 56 percent were institutionalized. Of the 3.5 percent of 65 to 74-year-olds who were dependent, 60 percent were still in the community.

Another large survey found that there are twice as many bedbound or housebound elderly in the community as in institutions, making up 10 percent of the noninstitutionalized elderly;[39] another 6 percent or so of those in the community could go out only with difficulty. On the other hand—to keep all this in perspective—the great majority of those over 65 have little or no impairment.

It's not completely clear how many of the impaired elderly in the community actually receive the help they need with personal care and how many simply suffer. The largest data set on the actual receipt of in-home help is from 1966–68, from special items in the National Health Survey. It showed that about 8 percent of the noninstitutionalized elderly received help from someone with moving about, bathing, dressing, and similar personal care tasks.[40] A Massachusetts study found 13 percent relying on other people in these areas to some extent,[41] while another 5 percent were judged to have an unmet need for such help.

The General Accounting Office estimated that the value of services provided by family and friends to each "extremely impaired" person in 1976–77 was $673 per month, exceeding then-prevailing nursing home rates.[42] These elderly used many fewer services from formal agencies, an average value of $120. The "greatly impaired" in the community also received greater value in services from family and friends than from formal agencies.

Before generalizing about the strength of the "informal support system," however, it is important to understand clearly what it consists of. These and other studies show that a majority of all the care comes from spouses. Of the rest, the largest part comes from middle-aged daughters and daughters-in-law,[43] much less from other relatives and very little from friends. Most care comes from relatives within the household. One observer has characterized the so-called "family support system" as a euphemism for female children and in-laws.[44] The strain of care, particularly for relatives who hold jobs, can be extreme: studies report stress-related illnesses, job interruptions, depression, fatigue, fear of the consequences of further dependence, guilt, conflicting demands on time, and family strife.[45]

Especially where income is low, caretaking families also experience financial pressures. Lower-income caretaking families need at least occasional substitute caretakers—whom they usually can't afford—and some financial relief. Tax credits and "respite" programs for substitute caretakers could help. It would be a mistake to believe that the "family support system" can be taken for granted or that it can pick up the slack from budget cuts. Further, many of the elderly, particularly those who now use long-term care programs, have neither spouse nor capable children. Since impairment is most frequent in the late seventies and eighties, it's not uncommon that the children of an impaired elderly are themselves aged, perhaps feeble. We need to be quite cautious about glib assumptions of the strength of informal supports.

In 1966–68, receipt of family care was inversely proportional to income and was half again as common for nonwhites than whites.[46] Over this two-year period, the frequency of family care declined, especially in the 65–74 age group where it went down by 12 percent.

Family Decisions and Health Crises

Publicly funded home-care programs have expanded considerably, but they're still small compared to the nursing home system. Most such programs have severe limitations on the scope of services provided, and most require "spending down" to virtually the welfare level for eligibility. This is an option which may not be possible, especially for an older person locked into a rent higher than such a budget permits. Furthermore, cuts in 1981 and later in federal block grants to states for social services (Title XX), which have funded most of these programs, augured recurring reductions, especially for those just above the Medicaid level. Often, when severe impairment strikes, the choice is between moving in with a child or a nursing home. This is seen as a Scylla and Charybdis choice— thinking about it evokes discomfort, avoidance, and denial. In the Rainwater-Bane interviews, one man whose mother is 89 said only "I hope not ever" and "I just don't know" to questions on whether a nursing home or more day-to-day care would be needed in the future. The nursing home is feared:

Only if it became imperative, because I could not do things for myself. But that would be the last straw. I would do almost anything to stay out of one. I would just hate it. I don't even want to think about it.

I'd feel this was really the end.

I'd never care for that. But in the same respect I wouldn't want to be a burden to my own children.

If I had lost my mind, become senile. That's the only way I'd allow it—No! No other way! *How would you feel?* I wouldn't feel anything. I'd

81

be out of my mind—I wouldn't know what was happening. Otherwise I'd hate it and whoever put me away.

Oh my God—that would really be the last straw. There is no humanity there.

Never—I'd rather live less years and die fast ... I hate nursing homes—I hate them with a passion. I hope I never have to—they don't care for you—they are only interested in the money they get.

Some respondents, however, took a more philosophical attitude. As between the nursing home or living with children, nonretired respondents whose preference could be discerned were approximately evenly divided:

I don't think I'd object if I could afford it—at least it wouldn't put too much of a burden on my children.

I wouldn't want to be a burden on other people. I don't think I would enjoy it but if you have to move to one, you have to.

If I'm incapable of caring for myself, then it would have to be—I would have no choice. I don't think that there would be much I could do about it.

If I had no other choice, then I would have to. The nursing home is the only place that can give constant care. If I needed that kind of care I would accept the idea. I'd be happy if that was what was required of me.

I would not like it at all, but I would make the best of it so I wouldn't be a burden to anyone.[47]

Care within the family is also seen as difficult for everyone concerned. It violates expectations of independence on the part of both generations and creates conflicts around issues of dependency. When combined with the genuine concern and sense of obligation that most children feel for their aged parents, this creates a difficult, emotional, and anxiety-producing dilemma in the families of the aged. Guilt is likely no matter what choice is made. The Census Bureau, in its study of long-term care, found that family conflict was frequent prior to placement of an elderly relative.[48] Another survey found that in two-fifths of households shared with the elderly, care of the older relative amounted to a full-time job.[49]

Differences in attitudes, preferences, and habits which are no problem at a reasonable distance can become major irritants in a shared home. A larger problem can be the difficulty of both generations in changing parent-child roles shaped over a lifetime. Often children have had to struggle to break free psychologically from the parental home. Consider Joseph Heller's caricature in *Good as Gold:*

Oh, Pa, I'm forty-eight goddam years old . . . I'm a college professor and have a Ph.D. I write books. I go on television. I get paid for making speeches at colleges and conferences. And you still talk to me like I'm a child. . . .

You got children, don't let them send you to Florida. The old shouldn't be with just the old. The old should be with the young, but they don't want us no more.

"Tell me, how is it that a father can take care of seven children, and seven children . . . can't take care of one father?" Gold . . . did not enumerate for him that the wise Yiddish folk proverb traditionally made reference to a mother rather than a father, that the posturing, melodramatic old f——k had never been able to provide for anything close to seven children at one time, and that his children *had* been supporting him.[50]

Many of the Rainwater-Bane respondents appeared to have never thought seriously about what would happen if their parents or in-laws were incapacitated. One man who visits his father in a nursing home two or three times a week nevertheless seemed to have no thoughts to express as to whether his mother might ultimately need similar care. Other responses:

It depends on the circumstances. It's hard to answer. Can't see into the future.

It's a possibility. I would imagine they would feel very badly about it and so would we—but it would have to be done.

I'd rather my wife took care of them [parents-in-law]. I wouldn't like it if they had to live in a rest home.

Not anytime in the foreseeable future—I don't know how I feel. *Parents were 80 and 81.*

Do you foresee a time when more day-to-day help will be needed? Who knows? *Parents deceased, in-laws 75 and 85.*

More day-to-day help? We just don't know. Fortunately their health is holding up. *Nursing home?* I hope not ever. *Mother is 89, mother-in-law in 80s.*

Foresee more help needed? Maybe—I haven't thought of it. *What would you and spouse have to do?* We've never thought about it before.

Many responses were simply "don't know." Some expressed willingness to take care of parents or in-laws themselves. On the whole, however, the impression was that few people had actually made plans for the contingency of a need for care, and that it would present a major dilemma for them.

The elderly themselves typically reject the coresidence option as interfering with their own freedom. Sometimes it seems, however, that they would feel differently if they thought they were welcome.

They don't want me. They told me right up and down. The daughter-in-laws don't want me. *But would you like it?* It's impossible, they have no room for me. I would say yes and no because they don't want me. The wives don't want me. They're the boss. *But you'd like to, if you could?* Yes.

Under current public policies, caring for an aged relative at home is much more of a financial burden to a family than arranging for a nursing home placement.[51] In the latter case, the total cost will be greater, but it will be paid by Medicaid once the older person's assets are spent. Most families caring for aged relatives at home, however, receive no public help, either financially or in services.[52] In fact, the older person's eligibility for benefits such as Supplemental Security Income or food stamps may be adversely affected.

Chronic Excess Demand and the Placement Game

The discussion earlier in this chapter sought to "account for" increases in the numbers of people in nursing homes in terms of changes in the size of population groups at risk, shifts from other forms of care, changes in the availability of informal care resources, and other predictors of need for care. This concept assumes, however, that supply ultimately follows demand. The relationship has come to be less true as state certificate of need programs are enacted and more strongly enforced, and as regulators use their control over total supply to the private and public markets to limit future Medicaid costs. In fact, beds built do tend to be beds filled whether in Minnesota, with 117 beds per 1,000 elderly, or in West Virginia with 16.[53]

Nursing homes are thought of, financed, and regulated as medical institutions. Actually, there is a world of difference between a hospital and a nursing home. A nursing home really is a place to live which provides help with the basic personal functions of daily life. Relatively little of the activity there involves sophisticated medical or nursing interventions—one reason why most nurses much prefer to work in hospitals, and why the best tend to do so. In seeking to control costs, officials have defined the problem as a technical one, following the medical model. They have frequently focused on assessment methodologies in their search for answers, borrowed from hospital utilization review approaches. The hope is that if publicly paid patients who "do not need to be there" can be kept out, the cost increases can be restrained.

The Congressional Budget Office (CBO)[54] summarized the results of fourteen studies of the appropriateness of placement in nursing homes. Estimates of inappropriate placement ranged from 10 to 70 percent, and the CBO concluded that 10 to 20 percent of skilled nursing facility patients and 20 to 40 percent of intermediate care facility patients were inappropriately placed.

Such estimates, however, are fundamentally arbitrary, because they must rely on an implicit judgment as to what kind of alternative care is available, in order to determine a level of disability at which care in the facility is "appropriate." Many of those judged in such studies as "inappropriately placed" do not actually have alternative care available to them, while many if not most of those judged appropriate could be cared for outside a nursing home with sufficient personal care.

The vast majority of patients in nursing homes, even skilled homes, are chronically impaired elderly who need help with the basic activities of daily living—bathing, dressing, eating, ambulation. *Most* such patients could in principle be cared for at home, with paraprofessional or family help and perhaps with some nursing supervision. One study that compared nursing home and home health patients found that the difference was not their level of disability, but the availability of social supports.[55]

The major constraints are the availability and willingness of family members or public authorities to provide constant care, and the choice of the patient and family. Those patients in nursing homes judged not to need institutional care would generally require some personal care in the home; unless such care were actually available the judgment is chimerical.

For those patients judged to need institutional care, but at lower levels, hypothetical cost savings could also be illusory. As with hospital rates, the rate paid for care of a given patient does not necessarily correspond with the actual cost of caring for that patient. Given a particular level of nursing and other resources available, elimination of less disabled clients from a facility would spread the available resources more thinly, resulting in either less extensive care or the need to add staff and increase rates. Since the freed beds might be filled with more seriously disabled, previously unserved patients, total costs could increase instead of decreasing.

In the search for the holy grail of cost control, a variety of forms and systems have been developed for assessment of prospective patients. These efforts have had relatively little success, for several good reasons. First, the problem is not really a technical one. Second, in order to avoid the costs of in-person evaluations, most of these systems have involved a paper review of forms, originally filled out in most cases by someone with a vested interest in having the placement approved— either a nurse in a hospital that wants to discharge the patient or someone from the nursing home itself. Third, there is no consensus as to what constitutes appropriateness for nursing home placement.

Several different approaches have been taken to the latter problem, some becoming entangled in litigation. New York's DMS-1 form gives points for various impairments and special care needs, based on a discriminant analysis of the differences between samples of actual skilled nursing facility and intermediate care facility patients.[56] Sixty points qualifies for an intermediate care facility, 180 for a skilled home. There turns out to be relatively little correlation among the ratings produced by the various assessment systems in use.[57]

There is an even more fundamental reason why preassessment screening for cost control has not been much of a success, and this goes to the heart of the problems of equity and access in nursing homes. A large proportion of nursing home patients enter facilities on a self-pay basis and then apply for public funds when their resources are exhausted. Self-pay patients typically convert to Medicaid within a year or two,[58] and private pay conversions often represent a major portion of nursing home residents supported by Medicaid. For example, in a South Dakota survey 30 percent of the Medicaid patients in homes at the time of the study had originally been admitted as private pay patients. For two-fifths of these, it had taken less than a year before their resources were exhausted and they converted to Medicaid; for more than another fifth it took one to two years.[59] A study of a sample of forty homes in the Detroit area found that 48 percent of residents had entered originally as self-pay patients, but that 66 percent of these were on Medicaid by the time of the study. Thus, about a third of all the patients were Medicaid conversions.[60] In a Monroe County, New York, study, the average time before private resources ran out was even shorter: 41 percent of conversions took place within six months of admission and 62 percent within a year.[61]

Politically and legally, self-pay nursing home admissions are usually considered private transactions; yet this is a major path from which Medicaid patients come. Once in the home, it would be both inhumane and impractical to force the patient out, and in a practical sense assessment screening does not usually apply to them. Sometimes they have been forced into lower levels of care, but uprooting fragile patients from an environment they have adjusted to is traumatic. (Some studies have claimed to show that "transfer trauma" has a significant effect on mortality, but the preponderance of the recent evidence does not support this argument, at least for properly planned moves.)[62] Attempts to move patients to a lower level of care, on the basis of the DMS-1 assessment, resulted in an injunction in a New York class-action suit, *Yaretzki v. Blum.*

Cost control policy for nursing homes is indeed a dilemma. Considering the revulsion against nursing homes described above, it would seem that no one would much need to be deterred from going there if other alternatives were available. (What happens to disoriented clients being placed from hospitals is another question.) But demand does seem to rise inexorably beyond the ability to pay for supply. It can be argued that admission screening, if it could be made to work, would result in fairer allocation of scarce nursing home beds in closer relationship to need.

The approach to cost control used by regulators thus far, however, has relied mostly on limiting bed approvals, creating a shortage of supply relative to demand, without dealing much with the mechanisms of access, especially for self-pay patients. Rigid application of certificate-of-need processes and the holding of Medicaid rates below private rates contribute to what one study[63] calls a "state of excess demand in equilibrium." Using this method of cost control, for lack of a better way, has all sorts of perverse side effects. Nursing homes can admit whom they choose, subject only to admission screening or utilization review procedures, if any, for initially-Medicaid patients. In a seller's market, they become selective. They tend to select against "heavy care" cases and those who cannot pay for at least the initial part of their stay through Medicaid.

The effect is that Medicaid subsidies are available to the more middle-class elderly who have resources and are initially ineligible, while they are not available to the "truly poor." Medicaid patients wait longer for placement: one recent study found they waited 50 percent longer than others in hospitals.[64] They may be placed far away from family and friends. As shown above, location is considered less often in nursing home placement for black patients, who are much more likely to rely on Medicaid from the beginning. They often must take the only facility available, and they receive fewer visitors. The proprietary homes that patients already on Medicaid can get into are often of lower quality and have lower rates than the better facilities, often voluntary, in which the more prosperous aged "mature into" Medicaid eligibility. Some Medicaid patients may not get into nursing homes at all. Studies by the federal government and other organizations find that in most places there is no real "shortage" of beds for self-pay patients, even while there is a severe "shortage" for the Medicaid patient.[65]

At best, getting into a decent nursing home, sometimes into any at all, is a complex business,[66] like getting a child into a good college. When beds are tight, it becomes much harder. In these situations, the availability of an effective advocate becomes crucial—and this role is typically played by the children of the middle-class elderly.

Chronic excess demand also means that nursing homes become exceedingly difficult to regulate. It is very hard to close an inferior home when there is literally nowhere to place the patients.[67]

Another perverse effect of maintaining a chronic shortage of supply relative to demand is delay in discharges of patients who no longer need acute care and are waiting for a nursing home bed. A New York study concluded that such delays cost the state $100 million a year.[68] In certain hospitals in the state, as many as one-third of the beds were occupied by discharge-ready "alternate care" patients at any given time, while 15 percent was not an unusual figure in major metropolitan hospitals. Medicaid patients waited an average of more than two months in hospital beds. This problem is a national one: a federal survey found that on a sample day in 1980, 6.6 percent of Medicare and 8.1 percent of Medicaid patients in hospitals were awaiting nursing home placement.[69]

These kinds of problems are the result of a system in which the question of "gatekeeping" is not addressed directly, yet there is unwillingness to pay for all the care that is demanded. The amount of care the public is willing to pay for may well be less than demand, but leaving rationing to the processes we have described has unfair and counterproductive side effects.

The perversities governing access to nursing homes raise serious problems of basic public policy and pit competing political values against one another. During periodic scandals (but seldom at other times), the proprietary domination of the industry is questioned. But "creaming" of patients, ethnic and cultural discrimination, and the like are also engaged in by voluntary nursing homes. (Both sorts are likely to defend themselves from the "creaming" charge by arguing that Medicaid rates provide insufficient reimbursement to serve "heavy care" patients.) The problems of the nursing home system raise the basic question of the control of a publicly financed, scarce resource by nonpublic providers with their own agendas.

The Growth of Publicly Sponsored Home Care

Long-term care in the United States has historically been dominated by the institution. In 1958, in a sample week, it was reported that only 701 elderly were receiving homemaker or visiting housekeeper service in the entire United States.[70] In the mid-seventies, more than 90 percent of public long-term care expenditures still went to institutional care.[71] There is no inherent technical reason for this institutional dominance. Experience in Europe,[72] and in some states and cities in the United States, has shown that home care can provide adequately for patients just as impaired as those in nursing homes, at a cost per day lower than or comparable to that of the institution. In the past it has been simply a matter of legislative and policy choices, federal and state, to exclude home care for the most part from the major health programs that finance nursing homes.

The reasons these choices were made are not completely clear. They should be seen in part in the context of historical American attitudes toward institutions. From the reform school to the mental hospital, institutions went through phases in which they took on a special aura. They were seen as workshops of experts at a salutary distance from society, where social problems could be solved efficiently through the division of labor, removal of "problem people" from society, and the disinterested expertise of professionals.[73] In the fifties, some sociologists spoke of the benefits of institutional care for elderly whose dependency needs might be hard for the family to handle, in a tone we would not expect to hear today.[74] But the institutional bias in long-term care really has had more to do with the medical model of care, and most of all with very real fears about costs.

There is a built-in disincentive to the use of nursing homes. Just as people usually subject themselves to surgery only when convinced it is needed, hardly anyone goes into a nursing home if he feels there is an acceptable alternative. There is no such disincentive for home care. In fact, help with household maintenance is a key part, in some cases all, of home care, and almost anyone, disabled or not, would appreciate having this. The potential rate of take-up among those eligible can be much higher than for nursing homes. Policymakers have long known of the large reservoir of severely impaired elderly not in nursing homes and have been unwilling to take it on. Even though the per-person cost of home care averages considerably less than nursing homes, creating home care benefits probably increases total expenditures since more people will be served.

Medicare administrators, especially, were at pains from the start of the program to strictly limit the large potential costs. Medicare does provide a home health care benefit, but policymakers took care to cast this benefit in a short-term, acute care oriented framework. This has insulated it from the large potential demand, which is for long-term support in making up for the infirmities of chronic disease. This means household care, shopping, and help with basic personal tasks of daily life like ambulation, dressing, and bathing.

The most important Medicare restriction has been the "skilled nursing requirement." The patient must be in need of "skilled nursing care," which by administrative definition is restricted almost entirely to time-limited situations like training a

The Growth of Publicly Sponsored Home Care

family member to perform procedures or to extremely specialized care. Other rules prohibit care which is considered merely "homemaking" and restrict the number of hours per week which can be provided. Rules limiting the number of days of care permissible per illness were liberalized in 1980 as a result of legislation, but a countervailing regulatory change in 1981 increased restrictions on the hours per week permitted. Despite all these limitations, Medicare spent about $630 million on home health care in 1980, almost five times the $133 million spent in 1974.[75]

In spite of the cost problem, care at home is a common-sense and more humane alternative to forcing the impaired aged into institutions. It is very strongly preferred by the elderly as well as their families. No matter how good a nursing home may be—and most are not particularly good—an institution inevitably takes away much of a person's freedom to make choices about the use of time, the living environment, and personal habits. The institution's procedures and its staff—often poorly trained, frequently changing, poorly educated, sometimes brusque, even angry or hostile—take on great power in the resident's life. As older people put it, the freedoms retained by staying at home include:

Anything from smoking a cigarette when I please to putting out the light when I please to making a meal when I please.

The thing is, you are independent and you have privacy. In the nursing home, you have to follow their schedule.

We've still got our own way of cooking and dressing in the morning—there's no one to say you nay.[76]

Other old people refer to nursing homes as "jails." For people who have acquired the habits and possessions of a lifetime, especially women who may never have had exposure to collective living and who have a heavy emotional investment in maintaining their own homes, the psychological cost of moving to a totally unfamiliar, impersonal environment, with little control, without so much as one's own furniture and keepsakes, can be profound. The psychological syndrome of "institutionalization" involves passivity, disorientation, withdrawal, and learned helplessness. Passivity, in fact, is rewarded in institutions, and the overuse of potent tranquilizers to create a docile institutional population is a serious problem in some homes.

A sense of control over one's life and environment is strongly correlated with morale and mental well-being. There is no clear evidence of a mortality effect caused by institutionalization of the aged, and there is much less research on this than on transfers from one institution to another, but one study did report a higher rate of mortality as a result of nursing home placement.[77]

During the 1970s, with distaste for the nursing home solution increasing and institutional rates on the rise, pressures grew for home care, and state and local programs expanded substantially. The major source of funds that became available for these programs was federal matching reimbursement for "social services" under Titles IV and XVI—later combined into Title XX—of the Social Security Act. A source used by a few states was a "personal care" option under Medicaid. Most states, however, have provided only "home health" services under Medicaid, using models rather like the Medicare one. This may be changing somewhat as a result of 1981 legislative developments.

Titles IV and XVI were enacted primarily with the service needs of public assistance families in mind. They were seen as an alternative to the counseling, special grants, and other services provided under the former caseworker system, when that system was being phased out in favor of a "separated" income maintenance system administered by clerks. This shift left many displaced caseworkers on the staffs of public welfare agencies, often with a rather vague mandate to provide "services." It turned out that there was much more demand for concrete home care services by the aged and disabled than there was for counseling and the like by welfare families. Thus home care programs in the seventies benefited from the process by which displaced bureaucracies find new roles to maintain organizational survival—much as the March of Dimes did after polio was virtually eradicated.

Under Title XX and, to a lesser extent, under Medicaid, state level home care programs grew rapidly during the 1970s and early 1980s. California's program grew from $80 million in 1974–75 to $250 million in 1980–81, despite the pressures of Proposition 13, with close to 100,000 clients. New York City's program, mostly under Medicaid, grew from about $40 million in 1974 to more than $300 million in 1981–82.

As a society, we are beginning to move away from policies that force older impaired people into institutions simply because they are the only place in which public financial support will be available for basic personal care. This is a considerable advance in humane care for the aged. So far, however, the implementation of these programs has been extremely uneven. It has depended almost entirely on the willingness of states to provide a share of the funds, in the face of severe competition from poor younger families and others for limited social services block grant or Medicaid funds.

The advance in home care programs comes at substantial financial cost, since its availability increases the total long-term care case load. Not only is demand great, but it is easier to limit nursing home beds, which take years to build, than slots in home care programs. Home care programs become an add-on to existing inventories of nursing home beds, though arguably they permit freezes of bed capacity which would otherwise be difficult.

To some extent, the availability of home care programs substitutes for care by families. The extent of this substitution effect is very difficult, if not impossible, to measure. Typically, however, when home care is provided to a patient with family in the household, care is shared between the family and the home care worker. Either because of ceilings on the amount of care which can be provided, or because the availability of family help is taken into account in allocating care, the formal programs offered in most states do not entirely substitute for family help. This is especially the case in homes shared with family—where most informal care takes place. As compared with nursing home placement, therefore, the home care alternative in a given case is likely to elicit *more* family contribution, since, as we've seen, children and other extended family members do not typically pay for parents' nursing home care. Of course, not all home care patients would otherwise actually be institutionalized.

As home care programs expand, one problem of social and legal policy will be to define whether, and to what extent, family participation in care should be required. There is in fact an element of informal bargaining in many programs as to the division of responsibilities between the program and the family—families often freely continue to provide a substantial share. But this can be difficult legally and practically to push beyond a certain point. It has been suggested[78] that home care benefits should not be operated on an entitlement basis, but rather distributed through fixed-budget agencies that would provide care "disproportionately to persons who have no able or willing informal supports." Putting such an approach into practice can raise severe difficulties. How should ability or willingness be determined? Uniform standards would be impossible to apply and major inequities would ensue. Such Solomonic judgments have proven almost impossible to administer in many other social programs. There is a basic incompatibility between the particularistic world of family relationships and the more universalistic world of the state and its agents.

Some large home care programs under Title XX pay family

members directly to provide care to siblings, parents, even spouses. A Michigan survey found that 55 percent of providers for the more than 11,000 clients being served in 1976 were family members.[79] Eleven percent were children living with the client, and another 7 percent were children living separately. In California, family members have provided a major portion of Title XX-financed home care, and have accounted for as much as 70 percent of providers in some counties. The number of persons being paid to care for family members is in the tens of thousands, and annual payments to them in the tens of millions.[80] Family members also are providers in home care programs in other states. On a smaller scale, the Maryland Office for the Aging has developed a program which also pays families directly for care of disabled members,[81] through a mechanism outside the regular home care programs.

Another major policy problem, which we discuss below, is the appropriate source of funding and financial eligibility criteria. One way to have equal access for the elderly, not based on geographical accident, would be to expand the care provided under the universal, non-means-tested, and fully federally financed Medicare program. Meaningful liberalization of the Medicare benefit would be enormously expensive, since *all* the impaired aged without regard to financial status would be eligible. Wider implementation of benefits under Medicaid would be somewhat less costly, though still very expensive, but the required "spend-down" of 100 percent of income above the welfare line would impoverish anyone who made use of the benefit. New legislation taking an intermediate approach would be the most appropriate (see chapter 7). The key principle, in achieving a balance among equity, adequacy, and cost control, would be an income-related sliding scale of contributions toward the cost of care, which would be substantial for middle and upper-income patients but which would leave enough income to afford food, housing, and other necessities at an adequate level.

Currently, it appears that the swing of the pendulum is away from the nursing home and toward in-home alternatives. With an appropriate legislative framework, it is possible to fashion benefits that offer meaningful alternatives to the nursing home, take some pressure off overburdened family caretakers, and bring care to many previously unserviced elderly. We need to realize, however, that we can never separate these effects perfectly, and some aggregate increase in costs is almost impossible to avoid. With the dislike for nursing homes, their high cost, the competing demands on potential family caretakers, and the desire of many elderly for independence, it is probable that home care programs will grow—as, on balance, they should. Nursing homes may not go the way of the orphan asylum, but they are likely to play a less central role in the long-term care system of the future. The challenge will be to find more comprehensive ways of planning and funding long-term care at all levels, institutional and community, to channel patients to appropriate and least restrictive levels of care, and to finance the programs in a way that avoids, on the one hand, spreading a limited benefit thinly over the elderly at all financial levels and, on the other, requiring their total impoverishment before eligibility.

The Future of Long-Term Care for the Elderly

Virtually all the major factors that are associated with demand for long-term care can be expected to increase in coming years. The population in the high-risk age groups will increase much faster than the total population or the numbers of persons 65 and older. Between 1980 and 2030, the number of persons 75–84 has been projected to increase by 140 percent and the number 85 and older to nearly triple.[82] If utilization within age groups remained the same, there would be a 54 percent increase in the number of nursing home residents by the end of the century and 132 percent, to almost 3 million, by 2030 when the large postwar generation reaches old age.

Other trends will add to the increase in demand. The proportion of the elderly who have a spouse to provide care will decline. Over the next twenty years, the number of widowed aged will increase by 33 percent, and the number of single aged by about 20 percent, while the number of married elderly will probably increase by somewhat less than 20 percent. Even more women will be in the labor force and unavailable for informal care; the participation of women in the civilian labor force is projected to rise from 48 percent in 1977 to 57 percent in 1985 and to over 60 percent by 1990.[83] The number of children the average older person has had will remain stable in the next twenty to thirty years, but when the postwar generation reaches old age it will reach a new low.

As potential demand for long-term care goes up, there will be proportionately fewer working-age people to pay the cost. The ratio of elderly to working-age people, which was at 18 percent for 1976, is projected at 26 percent for 2020 if fertility increases to replacement level, and 27 percent if it remains below that level.[84]

How will society handle these demands? It is not at all clear that all this potential demand will actually be met, at least not through expansion of nursing home beds. In fact, it appears that the increase in beds may have already slowed to less than the rate of increase in high-risk populations, although home care has expanded. Institutional and noninstitutional long-term care, taken together, may possibly keep up with the demographic trends. The real crunch, as with Social Security, will take place when those now in their thirties, and then those now in their twenties, begin reaching old age. These people may well overcrowd available long-term care resources when they reach old age, just as they overcrowded other institutions at earlier life stages.

The United States will get something of a preview from experience in Europe, where population structures are maturing earlier. In West Germany, the proportion of elderly has already reached 16.2 percent, following rapid increase in the 1960s and 1970s. Institutional long-term care beds were rapidly increased—old age homes by 25 percent and nursing homes by 75 percent—during the sixties. This still was not enough to absorb the increased demand, and the proportion of aged in these facilities fell slightly.[85]

Expansion of long-term care resources probably lies ahead, but it seems likely that the institutional sector will be extremely constrained in its growth while community care alternatives will be cautiously allowed to expand. The trend away from institutions could even parallel developments in the care of the mentally ill, where strong growth in the first half of the century was halted and then reversed as institutional care went out of fashion, though such a dramatic reversal is unlikely. The level of pressure which will exist on bed supplies will depend in part on the extent to which home care programs are allowed to grow. Given projected declines in the real value of social service block grants to states, this in turn may depend heavily on the extent to which personal care programs under Medicaid are permitted to grow.

Legislation in 1981 permitted states to expand home care and related services under Medicaid, including such ancillary services as case management, respite care, transportation, and the like, under a plan to be approved by the Secretary of Health and Human Services. Several states developed plans for major expansion of home care under Medicaid—California's would have shifted three-quarters of its program to Medicaid. The long-awaited shift to a less institutionally biased long-term care policy could emerge through these provisions. However, this may not be consistent with Federal efforts to cut the cost of Medicaid, and it may not be permitted to happen once federal policymakers realize that it is probably impossible to reduce *total* long-term care costs by providing alternatives to the institution.

At the federal level, long-term care has tended to be viewed as an intractable problem, and no clear sense of policy direction has yet emerged. A multistate "channeling" demonstration, developed at the end of the Carter administration, is testing what amounts to nursing home diversion programs.[86] While diversion programs have potential, the complex dynamics of the system we have described suggest that the channeling projects may have limited success. Few people, as it is, go into nursing homes if other resources appear available. The potential of screening systems of all kinds will be limited as long as a major route to Medicaid-funded nursing home care is the exhaustion of assets of patients who entered on a self-pay basis. Nursing home and home care admissions processes do need to be more closely linked. Perhaps the greatest potential for minimizing inappropriate use of nursing homes lies in strengthening hospital discharge planning operations, linking them more closely with local departments of social services or other agencies which are responsible for the authorization of home care. Hospitals need to be provided with incentives to carry out the more complex and time-consuming tasks of arranging for a package of care at home and follow-up care, rather than simply arranging a nursing home placement.

The complexities of the long-term care system pose tremendous obstacles to the plan proposed by the Administration in 1982 to take over Medicaid as a federal program, while turning public assistance programs over to the states. Leaving aside the difficulties involved in state financing of these latter programs on the declining revenue base offered to them, it would be extremely difficult to implement a federal takeover of the varied long-term care programs of the various states. As we've noted, close to half of Medicaid funds now go to long-term care, about 90 percent to the elderly. Nursing home rate structures, eligibility procedures, bed supplies, certificate of need processes, provision of home care under Medicaid, and many other aspects of long-term care vary greatly among the states. In principle a national standard might be very desirable. In practice, it would be tremendously difficult to bring about the kind of uniformity in entitlement which would be expected of a federally operated program—especially while simultaneously trying to reduce the Medicaid budget. A federal takeover of Medicaid, without more fundamental health systems reform, would pose enormous problems.

In any event, we are likely to be living with a state of "excess demand in equilibrium" for nursing homes for some time to come. This will mean increased attention to the side effects: hospital backup, difficulty in placing "heavy care" cases, and discrimination against patients without funds of their own. Nursing homes will remain a scarce resource, which means that access to them will be rationed in some way—if not by choice, then by chance, and in accordance with many private agendas and differences in access skills. We will need to look more critically at the processes by which people enter nursing homes and other forms of long-term care, and consider how to address the problem of privately controlled access to scarce and publicly supported care. Ultimately, although it *will* involve higher costs, there is a strong case for a nationally financed home care entitlement, administered locally on an eligibility model intermediate between Medicaid and Medicare.

In making the important policy and program choices for long-term care, we will be better off moving away from the medical models and hospital analogies which have dominated regulation and planning in this area. Long-term care is a social as much as a medical problem.

5

Catch-65: The Biased Pension Lottery

IN 1975, 7 percent of gross national product was spent on retirement income programs, more than five times the share in
1950.[1] The proportion probably is now well over 8 percent:
Social Security alone increased from 4 to 5 percent of gross national product between 1972 and 1982.[2] The proportion of the
aged population receiving income from a retirement program
increased from one-third to well over nine-tenths between
1950 and 1975.[3] These programs transfer income among individuals and among generations on a massive scale.

In pension policy, many of the themes we found in long-
term care recur: exploding costs, random and systematic inequity, ambiguity in defining government and nongovernment
roles. We do not have a coherent retirement income system,
but a patchwork of multiple, poorly articulated public and private benefits. As the costs increase, the talk is of "crisis," particularly for Social Security. Even under this fiscal pressure,
however, the issues are approached piecemeal. Pension policy

is largely a distributional issue, yet the public debate seems informed by little analysis of who gains, who pays, and how much.

Private and Public Sectors

The three main sources of aid to the aged are government, family, and private, employment-based benefits. Care of the chronically impaired, we found, is shared between government and family—private systems play a very small part. For income, the family has the small role; the major responsibility is shared by government and private benefit systems. Both for long-term care and for income, there is ambiguity about who should help: for long-term care it is between family and government roles, for income between public and private pension plans.

Private pensions, now a major factor, do not represent a preexisting system that was partially displaced by public benefits. As a widespread institution, the private pension system actually postdates Social Security. Extensive negotiation of private plans began in World War II, when they were used to compete for workers without violating wartime price controls. They expanded rapidly in the postwar boom years. The proportion of employees covered increased from less than 15 to 25 percent during the forties, and jumped to 41 percent during the fifties.[4] Since then, however, the growth has slowed: coverage was at 49 percent in 1975 and, as recent surveys show, has not increased since.[5] Thus just under half of private employees have plans available from which *potentially* they could earn a pension: as we shall see, these are, on the whole, higher income workers. Nevertheless, by any measure, these plans are a very important element in the total retirement income system. They account for about 17 percent of retirement benefits, while federal programs account for 76 percent, and state and local employee plans 7 percent.[6]

At the start, private pensions tended to be seen as an almost gratuitous undertaking of the company to reward loyal long-term employees and encourage commitment to the firm. As time went on, pensions became more and more a part of the total package on the bargaining table, and were increasingly recognized as a form of deferred compensation. As the scope of the system grew, the importance of the tax concessions increased, and the interrelationship between the private and public parts of the retirement income system became more apparent. Support grew for private pension regulation: initially, to provide for a minimum level of financial responsibility for fund trustees and to prevent the most blatant forms of preferential treatment for proprietors and managers.

Pension regulation in the United States, though it has increased, has not reached nearly the point that it has in some European countries, in which employer-provided plans are fit into a legislatively determined role in a total retirement system. Private pensions reach the greatest extent of public definition in countries where coverage by employers is fully or partially mandated and where vesting rules are strongest. In the United States, pension regulation followed precedents from regulation of financial institutions, concentrating on such matters as adequacy of funding and protection in the event of fund termination. Regulation was more gingerly when it came to rules that affect who gains and who loses, such as vesting principles.

The private system was left largely to its own devices until 1975, when the Employee Retirement Income Security Act (ERISA), widely thought of as a sweeping reform of the private pension system, was enacted. In fact, ERISA's innovations fell far short of fundamental pension reform, combining borrowings from banking regulation—notably, a federal insurance pool—with limited improvements in vesting requirements.

Through direct expenditures, taxation, and regulation, all the major components of retirement income can be seen as creatures of federal policy. Direct outlays for fiscal year 1982 include a minimum projection of $113 billion for Social Security retirement pensions; $35.5 billion for federal employee pensions; $5.8 billion for railroad retirement; and more than $4 billion in veterans' pensions. In proportion to overall federal direct spending on retirement income, pensions which are need-tested—through the Supplementary Security Income program—are small. At about $2.8 billion for fiscal year 1982, they account for less than 2 percent of the total. Theoretically, veterans' old-age pensions are also means-tested; in fact, there is a self-declaration system with little investigation of assets and no physical examination to determine disability.[7] Twenty-three percent of veterans over 65 receive such benefits. These expenditures are expected to increase dramatically in the 1980s as large numbers of World War II veterans reach retirement age.[8]

In addition to direct expenditures, federal policy supports retirement income programs indirectly through tax preferences. Private pensions could scarcely exist if they did not receive tax benefits. These permit payments to a pension plan on behalf of an employee to be tax-free, allowing it all to be invested and generate earnings which also are not currently taxed. Only when and as the pension is actually drawn is tax paid: usually at a lower rate, but, more important, after the money has generated many years of earnings. As the Senate Budget Committee has noted,[9] this has much the same effect as an interest-free loan, usually over several decades.

The Office of Management and Budget (OMB) computes "tax expenditures" in each year's budget, and they are very large. For 1983, they include $37.9 billion for the exemption of contributions to private pension plans and the interest on their earnings, $5.8 billion for similar treatment of individual retirement plans (Keogh and IRA), $2.4 billion for the additional tax deduction for the elderly, and $820 million for the exemption for capital gains taxation on the sale of a principal residence by a person 55 or older. The tax expenditure cost of excluding Social Security benefits for retired workers from taxation is estimated by OMB as $10.6 billion, with another $2 billion attributable to benefits for survivors and dependents.[10] Smaller but still substantial amounts are estimated for such subsidies as tax preferences on railroad retirement pensions and VA pensions, and the special tax credit for the elderly.

As we found in analyzing changing public attitudes, the growth of the public and private systems have both contributed to a shift away from expectations for family financial support. Chapter 3 showed that as Social Security and private pensions have grown, expectations have shifted from the family to these sources.

Social Insecurity

Social Security in the United States remains the heart of the retirement income system. By itself, it accounts for more than half the income of the median elderly person.[11] Because nearly all jobs are covered, credits are "fully portable" and most of the inequities resulting in other programs from job mobility are avoided.

Social Security is not, nor has it ever been, a simple forced investment comparable to an annuity. It is an extremely complex social program, financed from taxation on essentially a current basis, with provisions corresponding to a host of social and economic variations. Benefits are computed on social and political as much as actuarial considerations. Intimately involved in the economic lives of the vast majority of older people, Social Security policies reflect assumptions about such matters as the nature of the marriage partnership, divorce, and much else.

Social Security formulas represent a compromise between adequacy and proportional-return-on-contributions considerations. Thus, for a typical never-married retiree who earned the minimum wage, Social Security will replace 53 percent of his preretirement income, versus 28 percent for the worker who earned and paid on the maximum contribution.[12] For a married couple in which the husband had all the earnings, the percentages are 80 and 42 respectively (but less than this for a couple with the same income divided between two earners; see chapter 6). These skewed payoff formulas are a way of trying to consider adequacy as well as the amount contributed in benefit levels; but they are a very inexact and indirect way of reflecting need, since total retirement income is not considered. The "subsidy" to lower contributors is financed through the payroll tax, so middle-level employees contribute disproportionately to the subsidy while taxpayers with unearned income and income above the maximum subject to Social Security tax do not.

Benefits are not reduced by unearned income—such as private pensions or investments—while they are reduced by earned income. This controversial "earnings test" is defended as a way of encouraging savings while "insuring" against the loss of income caused by retirement.

Social Security has remained extremely popular compared to other government programs. Part of this, at least in the past, may have been due to the pride-maintaining illusion that the recipient is getting his own contribution back. The fact that past recipients typically received far more than their investment—even with interest—failed for a long time to spoil this illusion. But no miracle, or even clever investment strategy, was involved in this production of loaves and fishes. The high payoff resulted from population and coverage growth, and the shifting forward of obligations to future generations.

Consider a married man who retired at 65 in 1977. His maximum payroll taxes since the system's start in 1937 could not have exceeded $7705, with an equivalent contribution from the employer. Benefits to the employee and his spouse, at about $8400 for a maximum contributor, would exceed his contributions in the first year. Even more spectacular have been the payoffs to early participants in coverage expansions. Thus, someone who retired in 1950 under the newly implemented self-employment plan, and who lived until 1977, would have received $43,000 in benefits on an investment of $121.50.[13]

The mechanism which makes this possible is the time-honored principle of the chain letter or Ponzi scheme. In such a system, those who get in first profit greatly from the investments of those who join later. But there is always a day of reckoning. Future payoff rates will be considerably less beneficial. Future retirees—particularly single people, married women, and those who have paid the maximum tax—are likely to receive less in benefits than they could have received by investing their contribution on their own, in an Individual Retirement Account, for example. The worker retiring at 65 in 1997 would have contributed more than eight times as much as the 1977 retiree—$65,000 (matched equally by the employer). The benefits, however, would have increased by a factor of only three. The 1977 maximum-contribution retiree and spouse would have received benefits two-and-a-half times as large as they could have realized by investing his contribution privately,[14] while the 1997 retiree would receive benefits only two-thirds as large as could have been generated by individual investment. A single retiree would fare even worse.

As the financial problems of the system have become more visible, however, there is evidence that the public has now become acutely aware of its pay-as-you-go nature. In the 1981 Harris survey, 75 percent of the public understood that the Social Security taxes working people pay today are "used to pay Social Security benefits for retired people today," rather than being "set aside in a fund for their own future retirement."

While the covered population was growing, there was, in effect, a constant shifting forward of obligations onto coming generations. In 1945, 100 covered employees supported 2 in retirement; in 1955, they were supporting 12, and in 1965, 25. By 1975, the number had reached 31.[15]

The Social Security "crisis" is without doubt the best-known problem of old-age policy, although the near-term financing difficulty has been much exaggerated. In 1981, Reagan administration spokesmen, seeking substantial reductions in the way benefits are computed, made apocalyptic pronouncements of the impending bankruptcy of Social Security. They warned that without the proposed financing reforms, the money would be exhausted and "the checks could not go out" within a year's time. But actually, in 1981 there was a small surplus of revenue over outlays of $3.1 billion for the three Social Security trust funds combined. As we've seen, growth in the proportion of elderly will stabilize during the remainder of this century. Under the most pessimistic assumptions, the number of beneficiaries per contributor will only go up from the thirty-one in 1975 to thirty-four in 1995 and thirty-eight in 2005.

A revenue shortfall of modest proportions is projected for the eighties in the retirement trust fund, brought about mostly by higher unemployment rates than previously forecast. But borowing among the various Social Security trust funds has covered most of this short-term gap. The remaining shortfall would require, in the short term, only small adjustments, either through payroll tax increases, general revenue supplementation, or marginal benefit adjustments such as a change in the method of indexing (see chapter 7). Later in the 1980s, payroll tax increases already in law will help to balance the accounts. There is some truth in the charge that the administration used the threat of Social Security's near-term "bankruptcy" to try to achieve savings that would reduce the overall budget deficit.

The long-term problem, however, is much more severe: 73 retirees per contributor in 2035 under the most pessimistic assumptions, and 52 under "intermediate" assumptions. There is no getting around the fact that with 1.4 to 2 workers supporting each retiree something will have to give—much higher payroll taxes, benefit cuts, an advance build-up of the trust fund from its present token level to cover the problem years, or some combination of these. Still, it should be noted that today's benefit levels could be sustained even in the worst coming years if we were willing to pay social security tax rates at the level currently imposed in a number of European countries. The Dutch now pay combined employer-employee Social Security tax of 35 percent,[16] two-and-a-half times ours and more than we would probably need even under the worst conditions.

The social security ride will never again be almost free, at least not in any of our lifetimes. As we look at projected Social Security tax of a quarter or more of payroll, after generations of token contributions, and survey the prospect of curtailed benefits, a sense of betrayal is pervasive—who killed the goose that laid the golden eggs? The 1981 Harris survey found that 54 percent of all people 18 or over had "hardly any confidence" that Social Security would be able to pay them benefits when they retired, a dramatic decline in confidence from previous findings. The percentage was even higher among workers under 55, who face demographic storm clouds over their own retirement: for these the "no-confidence" figure was 68 percent. These findings are confirmed by the results of a New York Times–CBS poll, which coincidentally also found that 54 percent did not believe the money would be there to pay them their Social Security benefit.[17]

The Harris survey, however, found strong public opposition to Social Security cuts. Eighty-five percent opposed reducing benefits for future retirees, and 92 percent opposed any cuts for current retirees. Majorities opposed raising the retirement age for full benefits to 68, even gradually (59 to 35), supported raising Social Security taxes if necessary to provide adequate income for older people (51 to 39), and supported by more than two to one using income tax revenues to pay for part of Social Security (62 to 30). The only benefit reduction proposal that received public support (by 56 to 26 percent) was to base cost of living increases on either wages or prices, whichever is lower.

Some existing limitations on drawing Social Security, notably the "earnings test," draw substantial opposition. A 43 percent plurality favored allowing people to receive their full benefits no matter how much they earn on a job. Although a majority opposed "giving Social Security benefits only to elderly people who can prove they have little or no other income," 32 percent favored this change, which was hardly less popular than gradually increasing the retirement age. This suggests there may be strong support for less extreme ways of adjusting for need in the Social Security program, such as minimum benefits, higher replacement rates at lower earnings levels, and, potentially, taxation of part of Social Security benefits for those elderly at or above a comfortable income level. When asked in more general terms about most government programs to help the elderly, a majority of the public—51 to 43 percent—believed the programs should be available "only to those elderly who have little or no income."

Despite Social Security's problems, it commands strong support as the core of our retirement income system. The approval is even more impressive considering that the public far overestimates what it costs to run Social Security and far underestimates the percentage of contributions that finds its way into the pockets of recipients. A Roper poll found that the median public estimate of Social Security's administrative costs was $52.10 out of every $100 taken in, leaving less than $48 to pay benefits.[18] Even respondents with a college education estimated the expense at a median of $48.50, and only 2 percent thought that total administrative costs amount to less than 10 percent of the contributions collected. Actually, administrative costs in 1980 amounted to $1.50 out of every $100.[19] This compares extremely favorably with in-kind programs like Medicare and is dramatically better than private charities with their high fund-raising costs—or for that matter life insurance, annuities, IRAs, Keoghs, and other individual plans, which take out a much larger chunk for marketing and management. It plays well in Peoria for politicians to give the impression that federal social programs waste a large proportion of their revenues in administrative costs, but in fact the major federal income-support programs do remarkably well in this regard. Better public understanding of these issues might improve the reputation of universal, income-based strategies, as against service strategies or individual plans.

As with other aspects of old-age policy, the increasing cost of Social Security forces us to look more carefully at who benefits and who pays. Even more to the point, we need to look at how the different components of our retirement income system fit together.

Like the American socioeconomic structure, the retirement income system can be visualized in the shape of a diamond. Supplemental Security Income (SSI) constitutes the means-tested bottom layer, or floor, reaching relatively few. Social Security (Old Age and Survivors' Insurance) constitutes the large middle layer. The top layer is made up of private and government-employee pensions, and increasingly of tax-preferred, individual plans. While supported by government policy, this third layer aids a relatively well-off minority of the aged. Nevertheless, the private pension system, especially, has become an institution of crucial importance in the economic life of the aged, in the economy as a whole, and in regulatory, tax, and social welfare policy. When viewed systemically, private pensions raise serious issues of equity and adequacy. Since these issues have received less attention than has the problem of financing Social Security, the private system is discussed in some detail below.

Private Pensions: Growing Like Topsy

The private pension system has grown dramatically in the postwar period. The assets of these plans increased sevenfold between 1960 and 1979—from $52 billion to a remarkable $363 billion.[20] The growth of this system has been largely a creation of public policy. The Revenue Act of 1942 codified the long-term tax deferral that is at the heart of the system, by treating employer contributions to qualified pension plans as tax deductible, excluding plan investment income from taxation, and allowing benefits to be taxed only when received after retirement.[21] Labor legislation, as interpreted by the National Labor Relations Board and by the Supreme Court, notably in the U.S. Steel decision of 1949, established pensions as a mandatory subject of bargaining, a decision credited with an important role in benefit expansion.[22]

Coverage under private pension plans increased from 15 percent of the private, nonagricultural labor force in 1940 to 49 percent in 1975. Coverage is concentrated among large, unionized, and/or industrial employers. This "smokestack America" sector of the economy has been growing less quickly than the sectors where private pensions are less typical. The growth in coverage has stagnated in recent years, and there are few prospects under existing circumstances of covering a substantially larger share of the work force. It is expected that fewer than half of retirees early in the next century will have private pension income.[23]

The dramatic growth of the assets of private pension plans, as well as public employee programs, is shown in table 5-1. The growth of the 1970s is even more impressive considering

Private Pensions: Growing Like Topsy

TABLE 5-1

Assets of Private and Public Pension Funds

(Billions of Dollars)

Year	Private	State and Local	Federal	Total
1960	51.9	19.6	na	na
1965	86.5	33.1	na	na
1970	138.2	60.3	27.5	226.0
1971	152.8	69.0	30.4	252.2
1972	169.8	80.6	33.4	283.8
1973	182.6	84.7	35.5	302.8
1974	194.5	88.0	38.2	320.7
1975	217.4	104.8	41.9	364.1
1976	249.4	120.6	46.4	416.4
1977	283.0	132.6	52.9	468.5
1978	321.3	153.0	59.8	534.1
1979	362.7	178.9	67.7	609.3

SOURCES: American Council on Life Insurance (ACLI), *Pension Facts 1977* (Washington, D.C., n.d.), cited in James H. Schulz, *The Economics of Aging* (2nd ed., Belmont, Ca.: Wadsworth Publishing Co., 1980), p. 170; Securities and Exchange Commission, "Assets of Private and Public Pension Funds," from Federal Reserve System, ACLI, and SEC data.

that the prices of stocks, in which much of the assets are invested, fell considerably in real dollars (the Dow Jones average opened the decade at 800 and closed it at 838, while the Consumer Price Index increased by 84 percent). At the end of 1979, pension fund reserves were 16.2 percent as large as aggregate financial assets of households, up from 12.4 percent in 1970 and 3.4 percent in 1946. From 1970 to 1979, the aggregate assets of public and private pension funds grew at an annual compound rate of 11.6 percent while the Consumer Price Index increased by 7.6 percent per year. Annual employer contributions to plans went from $180 million in 1940 and $1.75 billion in 1950 to $23 billion in 1974.[24]

Actual pension *obligations* are much larger than these figures indicate. While pension fund reserves reflect the portion of pension obligations which are "funded"—for which the money has actually been set aside—a substantial part of pension fund

115

obligations are not funded in advance but are simply a liability of the company, a lien on future earnings estimated at $100 billion or more.[25] For many major corporations, unfunded pension obligations are a substantial proportion of their total net worth. By 1977, General Motors was estimated to have an unfunded vested pension debt of $3.5 billion, a fifth of its net worth. Ford's unfunded obligations, at $1.3 billion, were a third of its net worth. LTV, Inc., had unfunded obligations in that year amounting to 125 percent of its net worth.

As the size of the system has grown, so has the size of the tax subsidies it benefits from. By OMB estimates, the annual tax expenditure is projected to grow by 340 percent from 1977 (when it was $8.7 billion) to 1984.[26]

Private pensions go to workers with long continuous service in jobs that have such coverage. In general, these turn out to be higher income, relatively skilled positions, and the long-term workers in these jobs turn out to be mostly white males. The system is "one that serves men better than women, whites better than nonwhites, and higher paid, more stable workers, particularly in craft, managerial, technical, and manufacturing jobs, better than lower paid, less stable workers, particularly in service, clerical, and household jobs."[27] Not only is private pension coverage concentrated in better jobs, but less stable workers lose out on getting any benefits when they do not remain long enough for their entitlement to "vest."

The system functions as a sort of lottery. Long-term employees benefit both from the contributions made on their own behalf and those made on behalf of shorter-term employees: this makes possible substantial pension benefits at a lower cost to the firm. If only random factors differentiated the winners and the losers, as in a real lottery, the problem would only be one of adequacy. Since the groups differ substantially and systematically—by income, race, and sex, among other factors—the problem is one of systematic inequity as well. In this respect, though there is a random element, the lottery metaphor is inexact: it is more like a series of screens, which in this case separate the "men" from the "girls." (Or as Bernstein[28] put it, employees are camels and qualifying requirements are the eyes of needles.) First one has to be in covered employment, then one must attain vesting requirements. Once these obstacles are surpassed, there are also differences in the adequacy of benefits. All these differences are systematic.

Pension Coverage and Vesting

Differences in coverage represent the first "screen." In 1979 32 percent of women and 51 percent of men were covered.[29] Racial differences are comparable. A study of workers nearing retirement found whites more than twice as likely as blacks to have been covered by a pension on their longest job. In this study only 7 percent of nonwhite nonmarried women, versus 51 percent of white men, were covered.[30] Blacks are less likely to work in the kinds of jobs in which pension coverage is high.

Table 5-2 shows how private pension coverage and public-employee coverage (which is less income-dependent) vary with

TABLE 5-2

Pension Coverage by Income, 1979

Income	Percentage Covered
Less than $5,000	13
$5,000 to $10,000	38
$10,001 to $15,000	59
$15,001 to $25,000	71
More than $25,000	73

SOURCE: President's Commission on Pension Policy, *Coming of Age: Toward a National Retirement Income Policy, Final Report* (Washington, D.C.: Government Printing Office, 1981), based on analysis of U.S. Bureau of the Census Current Population Survey data.

the worker's income. High-income workers are far more likely to be covered.

In order to actually receive a pension, it is not enough merely to have worked in a job covered under a plan. It is necessary to work in that job long enough to acquire rights to the pension: this is referred to as "vesting," typically requiring ten years on the job. Those who leave before the minimum "vesting" period get nothing. In 1979 only 26 percent of workers actually had vested pension rights.[31]

The equity problems resulting from differential coverage are multiplied by those resulting from vesting requirements. Women are much more likely to be "in and out" of the labor force and much less likely to achieve the required length of service. Job tenure also differs by race and income level.

By Labor Department estimates, median tenure on the current job in 1978 was 2.6 years for women and 4.5 for men. Less than 16 percent of women had been on the current job for 10 years or more.[32] The trend has been toward shorter tenure; the median declined by 8 percent between 1973 and 1975. Among workers close to retirement age (55–64), the gap between men's and women's tenure increases, reflecting the interruption and recommencement of women's work activity because of family responsibilities. In this age range, median job tenure was well over the typical ten-year vesting requirement for men at 13.5 years, but was under it for women at 8.4 years. Tenure *at* retirement would be somewhat higher, but clearly there will be a substantial proportion of women who had not worked ten years at their current job when they reach retirement. Even among those who succeeded in vesting minimum rights in their last job, the average number of years of vested benefits as well as the average wage base for women will be smaller, producing large differences in pension amounts.

ERISA set some minimum standards for vesting of benefits. Several options were provided, with most employers opting for vesting of accrued benefits only after ten years of service. This degree of vesting has continued to leave out a large proportion of the work force, especially women, minorities, and low-paid workers, and does not appear to have materially altered the distributional effects of the system. The workers most in need of pension protection may not even come close to ten years' service with one employer. If they do, the pension from one such employer, with credits from other experience lost, is likely to be minimal—especially since when an employee leaves a job before retirement age, vested pension rights are not adjusted for inflation. Thus the pension from a job left ten or twenty years earlier is worth little. In spite of the ERISA vesting requirements, the only ones who really get much from the private pension system are those who not only work in covered employment but work for most of their careers, right up to retirement age, with a single employer.

Pension Receipt

The result of these patterns is that the typical private pension recipient is male, white, and retired from a relatively well paying position in a large corporation. In a study of the retired, 46 percent of the men and 21 percent of the women were receiving private pensions; for those women who did receive pensions, the average amount was less than half the men's.[33] Another study, this one of workers retiring from jobs where there was pension coverage, found that 48 percent of blacks and 23 percent of whites, though covered, nevertheless failed to actually qualify for a pension.[34]

The Senate Budget Committee, based on a Congressional Budget Office analysis,[35] found in 1978 that employees who benefit from tax expenditures for private pensions "are primarily middle and upper income taxpayers ... Lower income taxpayers also benefit proportionately less because a significant number of employer plans are integrated with the social security system." Only 5 percent of the tax expenditures subsidizing this system went to taxpayers in the $10,000 and under class, while more than 65 percent went to those in the $20,000 and up class. In one study, private pensions accounted for 15 percent of the total income of higher income married old people but less than 1 percent of the total for those with low income.[36]

"Integration" of plans with the Social Security system means that benefits from the private system can be reduced by the amount of Social Security received, or a portion thereof. The rationale is that under this approach a specific percentage of the worker's pre-retirement income will be replaced in retirement for each year of covered service. In fact, the system works to further concentrate pension benefits and the tax subsidies behind them on higher paid workers. Plans with "integration" (qualified under ERISA for tax benefits) are often set up so that retirees who earned less than the maximum amount subject to Socal Security tax get relatively little once part of their Social Security benefit is subtracted. The private pension will replace a much higher proportion of income that exceeds the Social Security ceiling. As one employer's handbook points out: "The integration of pension and profit sharing plans with Social Security is a concept which can allow you—as an employer—to create a pension plan which 'discriminates' in favor of your highly paid employees . . . [although] this may seem too good to be true."[37]

The distributional problems of private pensions are not unique to the United States. Tax subsidies on private pensions in Britain are somewhat similar, amounting to £2 billion per year.[38] The proportion of old people receiving private pensions is high among those who formerly held white-collar positions (more than 60 percent for managers and professionals and nearly 75 percent for other nonmanual employment), but drops to less than 50 percent among former blue-collar employees. The average British professional or managerial pension is five times that of the unskilled manual worker. Those least likely to receive private pensions, as in the United States, are those most likely to suffer social, medical, and economic privation—the old-old and the widowed, especially widowed women. Only 19 percent of widowed British women receive private pension income. Results are much the same in Canada: in 1971, 27.5 percent of men and 10.5 percent of women reported receiving private pension income.[39]

In the United States, a 1970 Social Security Administration survey indicated that for those fortunate elderly who did receive private pensions, these pensions replaced, at the median, 25 percent of pre-retirement earnings for men and 19 percent for women.[40] Replacement rates have increased since 1970, and of course are added to Social Security benefits and other income sources, producing reasonably adequate income replacement—of initially higher earnings—for this group. These replacement rates can be compared to findings on private pension coverage and replacement rates for average workers in five European countries in 1975.[41] The four plans studied on the Continent—Germany, France, the Netherlands, Sweden—all had higher coverage rates and lower replacement rates than either the United States or Great Britain.

The system in the United States, therefore, reaches less of the work force, but pays off better for the fortunate group that is covered. The French system, for example, mandates coverage by all but the smallest employers. However, this system provides only a low replacement rate, amounting to 8 percent of pre-retirement earnings for 1975 retirees who had been in the system for the 18 years since its creation, and 20 percent ultimately for those who put in 44 years. In the Netherlands, as in France, 80 percent of workers are covered, but benefits at maturity only provide 7 to 11 percent of earnings. These continental systems have provisions both for vesting and portability (the ability to transfer credits from one employer to another).

The British system did not (with some changes expected as the result of new legislation); it covered about 45 percent of workers, but provided a 23 percent replacement rate. Apparently, when fewer employees can qualify for pensions—because of partial coverage, stringent or nonexistent vesting provisions, or lack of portability—private systems provide more generously for those who win the lottery. Those who win the pot can divide up the antes of those who had to drop out of the hand.

Other Pension Programs

Public employee pensions and individual tax-subsidized plans (Individual Retirement Account and Keogh) are also large elements in the overall retirement income support system, and involve even greater equity issues. ERISA does not regulate public employee pensions, and their vesting requirements are usually worse than the minimum permitted under ERISA. Thus public plans suffer even more than private ones from the inequities brought about by the inability of many employees to vest their rights. Peter Drucker[42] characterizes typical public plans as a form of "involuntary servitude" bordering on peonage. Employees are effectively tied to the job for 15, 20, or even more years before they vest any rights. If they leave earlier, they lose all pension credits. Sometimes even a move to another department in the same city has this effect.

In the public employee lockstep, once the worker has a number of years in, he can scarcely afford to leave, even for an outside job which could make better use of his talents. On the other hand, once the career worker has 20 or 25 years in, it becomes profitable for him to retire in his mid-fifties, often at the peak of his ability and experience. American government workers, until they reach the state of vested grace, have less mobility than those in almost any other major country.[43]

Other Pension Programs

Even more than in the private world, public employees are sorted into big winners and big losers—and the big winners, those who work a full career in one public job, do remarkably well. A study of a sample of state and local plans found that those who retired at age 65 with 30 years' service received on average well over 100 percent of final salary in pension benefits.[44] The local plans provided for an average of 111 percent to 122 percent replacement, depending on the level of income. The newly retired "young-old" could therefore do extremely well. Older retirees often had benefits far less generous, since 59 percent of the plans had no provision for inflation, and only 2 percent were fully indexed to the Consumer Price Index. Given the contingencies of life which can lead to breaks in service, public pension plans seem to have more of the attributes of a lottery than of a planned, publicly supported retirement income system.

How does this happen? One answer is that the unions and other employee organizations that negotiate with public employers and lobby legislatures are more responsive to long-term employees, who pay close attention to their retirement benefits, than they are to the large number of more transient employees. As we find so often in public policy, interest in issues and the ability to be heard does not run parallel to need.

Public employee pension programs expanded vigorously in the sixties and early seventies. By the late seventies, the cost of these obligations became a major problem for government at all levels. In 1981 the cost of federal retirement programs reached $35 billion per year. Public employee programs are less likely to be fully funded than are private plans, in large part because they are unregulated. Unfunded pension obligations of some jurisdictions have reached remarkable levels—more than $2.5 billion in Los Angeles, for example, and $9 billion for the California State Teachers' retirement system, a figure projected to reach as high as $50 billion in the next 20 years.[45]

In 1981 the mayor of Los Angeles attributed major layoffs and reductions in the city's services to the cost of police and fire pensions coming due; these costs had increased 300 percent during the previous decade, amounting in 1981 to 76 cents for every dollar of salary. Unfunded pension costs resulted in a jump of 35 percent in expenditures in a single year—to $238 million for 1981–82.[46]

The unfunded debt of the federal pension system, however, even makes numbers like these look small. In the civilian employees' system, about 38 percent of payroll is set aside annually, but this makes the program less than 50 percent funded, since it has been estimated that 80 percent of payroll each year would have to be set aside to fund the obligations on an actuarial basis.[47] The military retirement system is on a pay-as-you-go basis; the requirement for full funding in this program, with its very early and lengthy retirements,* has been calculated at 100 percent. All together, the President's Commission on Pension Policy has estimated the unfunded actuarial liabilities of these two systems at no less than $750 billion, three-quarters of the national debt.[48]

Reform of public pensions, especially local and state ones, is unlikely in the absence of a Public Employees' Retirement Income Security Act (PERISA). Given the current condition of state and local budgets, under enormous pressures from federal cuts, reform would be a slow process. But progress is possible. The hard-pressed City of New York managed to reduce its unfunded pension debt by 10 percent between 1980 and 1981.[49]

Public pension reforms are needed both in vesting and funding. Such reforms would have a substantial short- and middle-term cost. However, there are several things to be gained in addition to equity for employees. Advance funding

---

* A 37-year-old military retiree writes to Dear Abby to complain that he can't properly enjoy his retirement years with his wife, since his being around the house all day drives her crazy. *The New York Post*, February 15, 1982, p. 30.

would improve the stability of state and municipal financing and, ultimately, the credibility of the bonds of these jurisdictions. It would prevent the undue passing along of obligations to another generation, make visible the cost of commitments as they are entered into, and, probably most important, provide new investment capital as the reserves of public pension funds increase. Reform of public as well as private pension funding could well contribute more to the reindustrialization of America than the tax and budget cuts touted by the "supply side" school; they would require a true reallocation from current consumption to investment.

Even more skewed to high-income taxpayers than the private pension subsidy is the tax expenditure for Keogh and Individual Retirement Account (IRA) plans. The amount of this tax expenditure was estimated by the Office of Management and Budget at $5.8 billion in the fiscal year 1983 budget. This was up from $3.7 billion in 1981, in part because of liberalization of IRA rules, and may turn out to be an underestimate.[50] Forty percent of such tax expenditures went to employees in the $50,000 and up income range,[51] according to a 1978 Congressional Budget Office estimate (a range comparable to the $70,000 and up bracket in 1982). Only 2.4 percent went to those in the $10,000 and under class.

Another government report found that of IRA eligible taxpayers in 1976, 45 percent of those with income over $50,000 and less than 1 percent of those with income under $15,000 took advantage of the program.[52] Similarly, the President's Commission on Pension Policy[53] found that in 1977 more than half of those with family incomes over $50,000 who were eligible for IRAs used them. In sharp contrast, far smaller percentages of lower-income eligible families used them, either because they could not spare the income or because the tax benefit is so much less at lower incomes. Of those eligible, only .2 percent of those with incomes under $5,000, 1.3 percent of those from $5,000 to $10,000, 3.3 percent of those from $10,000 to $15,000, and 5.5 percent of those between $15,000 and $20,000 had IRAs. As with employer pension plans, tax deferral provides the equivalent of a long-term interest-free loan to the predominantly high income taxpayers who use IRAs.

IRA benefits are directed to stated goals of income adequacy in retirement, like the more structured income security programs. Because they are individually activated, only those with disposable income use them heavily. The people who need retirement income the most simply do not take advantage of these programs. The tax benefit is greatest at high incomes because it is based on a tax deduction. The trend toward individually activated but tax-subsidized plans will divert large amounts of tax revenues while doing very little for the elderly who really need help.

The tax expenditure for IRA plans was increased considerably as a result of the extension of eligibility for IRAs as a third pension (on top of both a private employee pension and Social Security), which was part of the 1981 "Christmas tree" tax and spending cut package. There is no reason to believe that lower-income employees with private pensions will tend to use IRAs to any greater extent than lower-income self-employed and uncovered employees did before the change. By the mid-eighties, tax expenditures for IRAs can be expected to reach $10 billion or more annually. On the positive side, this may generate some needed increase in the national savings rate, but it will do so through a tax subsidy approach whose benefits will accrue overwhelmingly to higher-income people. Lower-income workers without private pension coverage have made little use of the IRA provision in the past, but it has made a marvelous tax shelter for upper-income self-employed professionals. These will now be joined in the millions by upper-income corporate professionals, managers, and skilled workers with company pension plans and discretionary income.

Misleading ad campaigns have much oversold the potential of individual plans to provide adequately for retirement. These ads inform us that one can become a near-millionaire at retirement through the miracle of compound interest, simply by putting $2,000 (the current ceiling for an individual) into an IRA each year. They use illustrative rates of 12 percent or so. What they don't say is that if interest rates are at that average level over the long haul, the rate of inflation will probably be in the range of 8 to 12 percent or even higher (in several recent years, inflation exceeded interest rates). The $600,000 which a $2000 a year contribution at 12 percent interest could build to, over 30 years, would be worth perhaps $75,000 in today's dollars, *if* interest rates manage to stay a little ahead of inflation. If there is a period of hyperinflation at some point in that span, all bets are off.

The publicity for IRA's is reminiscent of the old story about the man who recovered from a twenty-year coma. Released from the hospital, he called his bank, and was delighted to hear that his balance had grown to over a million dollars. Then the operator came on the line: "Please deposit $50,000 for the next three minutes. . ."

The Economic Significance of Pension Funds

The scale of pension systems is not always fully appreciated. In 1976, $119 billion was paid out in private and public benefits; this was ten times the amount spent on public assistance and $30 billion more than national defense costs.[54] Pension funds held six-tenths of a trillion in assets in 1979, and seven-tenths in 1980, the majority in private funds, which increased by a factor of more than two and a half between 1970 and 1979. These amounts are increasing much faster than the aggregate value of corporate equities: private pension funds own an increasing proportion of U.S. equity capital.

Each major policy and program for the aged has come to have unexpected consequences and functions, and pension funds are no exception. The funds have taken on importance beyond their income support purpose: they are a critical part of our economic system. A New York Stock Exchange study estimated that institutional investors held approximately 50 percent of the stock of companies listed on the Exchange at the end of 1980; and "institutional investors" means, predominantly, pension funds.[55] Drucker[56] has been one of the few to call attention to the importance of this. He characterizes the situation as "pension fund socialism," following the classical Marxist definition of socialism as ownership of the means of production by the workers.

Drucker argues that this state of affairs means that the incidence of the corporate income tax is far different than generally thought, suggesting that it has actually become an "exceedingly regressive" tax soaking the poor, since in large part it is a levy on the beneficiaries of pension plans. He argues that nothing would promote greater equality of income more effectively than eliminating it. This analysis, however, fails to take the inequitable distribution of pension claims into account: pension beneficiaries do *not* represent all the workers or even a representative sample of them.

Pension funds are an important source of capital for business; as fiduciaries they must invest conservatively. Some analysts believe that one factor in the decline in the growth of productivity in the late 1970s was the tendency of capital markets dominated by institutional investors—mostly pension plans—to play it safe, and avoid investing in high-risk, entrepreneurial enterprises and new technologies.[57]

Both private and public pension funds have the potential to create large amounts of needed capital. In the United States, Social Security functions essentially on a pay-as-you-go basis and so does not generate capital. In many other countries, public systems are "funded," and their existence creates a network of interests with vital concerns with pension policies. The Swedish National Pension Insurance fund accounted for almost half of total advances on the Swedish credit market in 1970–71, while the Canadian funds, controlled by the provinces, provide an essential element in provincial financing.[58] The provinces have been able to borrow from the funds at less than market rates, to an extent which amounted to 38 percent of all their borrowing in the early 1970s. Canadian sociologist John Myles suggests that in fact the Canada Pension Plan was created more for this purpose—as a vehicle for provincial economic development—than for its manifest function as an income maintenance program for the aged.[59]

Private pension plans, too, are important in Canada as in the United States. In either country, an expanded, universal public pension system could affect investment in private business by private pension plans, though if advance-funded it could create new offsetting capital (for example, by buying government bonds which would then not compete with private debt offerings). One study found that private pension plans in Canada were projected to furnish from 70–80 percent of all new capital raised by stock and bond issues for industry.[60]

In the United States, the private funds have come to play a crucial role in the financial system on a larger scale. Just as a "medical-industrial complex" has substantial vested interests in the health care of the aged, private pensions create a network of vested interests and policy considerations quite distinct from their manifest function. Insurance companies, banks, unions, and other institutions are vitally concerned with pension policy and derive profit and power from managing pension funds. (Insurance companies are also a crucial vested interest in health care of the aged, strongly opposing any national health proposals that fail to give them their share of the action.) When a giant insurance firm places public-service display ads stating that "Social Security was never *intended* to be more than a basic system supplemented by private pensions and individual savings,"[61] they do so from a position of considerable financial interest as a portfolio manager for billions in fund investments, as well as a vendor of products like IRAs and annuities which compete with Social Security.

But even without a diminution of the role of private funds, serious problems are likely to emerge in coming years with regard to their function in capital formation. To add to the capital stock, pension funds must take in as contributions more than they pay out as benefits. Through the 1970s, the funds did so. But demographic developments could change this.

When a society has a high proportion of workers to retirees, and is putting money away for the future retirement of the workers, capital is being created. But when the population structure matures, the creation may stop. Drucker projects that by 1985 or 1990, the balance will start to turn and the funds will become pure transfer mechanisms or even net dissavers, depleting capital stocks. As large cohorts of beneficiaries reach retirement, the funds will increasingly need cash income. They may "spend from endowment" for some period by selling securities. They may also slow another major source of capital formation, retained earnings, by pressing the companies whose stock they own—or collectively control in some cases—to increase dividends at the expense of retained earnings. This problem is really one more aspect of the "squeeze" that will result when a higher proportion of retired workers must be supported by smaller numbers of current workers.

There are many ways in which the capital formation problem can be solved in the coming decades, but all have zero-sum elements. If more resources are to be set aside for investment in the future—to create modernized industrial plants, to finance increased research and development, and to otherwise generate real economic growth—then contributions to pension funds will have to increase at the expense of salaries, or benefits paid to retirees will have to be restrained. Moves toward better vesting and/or mandated coverage would require larger contributions to pension funds and work against the slowdown of capital formation which may otherwise take place.

"My Helmet Now Shall Be a Hive for Bees":
Retirement Age

Improved pensions have, more or less intentionally, encouraged the elderly to leave the labor force. Pension rules have also encouraged retirement *before* 65, lowering the average retirement age. By Census Bureau estimates, labor force participation by men 60–64 declined from 83 percent in 1955 to 66 percent in 1975.[62] The President's Commission on Pension Policy estimated that in 1979 only 34 percent of men and women 60–64 were in the labor force.[63] Delaying retirement past 65 also is now less frequent: by Census estimate, worker proportions for men 65–69 were 57 percent in 1955, and 32 percent in 1975.[64] The President's Commission figured that in 1979 only 8 percent of all those over 65, men and women, were still in the labor force.[65]

In fact, it can hardly be said any more that 65 is the "normal" retirement age. Most new Social Security applicants are now retiring before 65: 77 percent of men and 79 percent of women in 1977.[66] Federal workers retire at an average age of 61,[67] and only 16 percent wait until 65.[68] The same trend is taking place in large corporations, encouraged by pension policies: a General Motors executive reports average retirement age in some recent years at as low as 58. In 1977 the average retirement age for police was 48 in Los Angeles and 49 in New York State.[69]

While the proportion of older people in the labor force has been shrinking, participation by non-elderly women, particularly married women in their middle years, has climbed. With the growing labor force, total employment has actually increased regularly, but so has unemployment. During the Depression, encouraging old people not to work was an explicit aim of public policy—it was a major goal of Social Security. It was felt that if there were not enough jobs to go around, the elderly ought not to be competing for them with the heads of young families. Some people still take this position.

In today's economy, however, there is little evidence that the withdrawal of the aged from the labor market really does much to reduce unemployment for the nonelderly. The labor market is highly heterogeneous by geography and by skills; some jobs remain unfilled even in the face of high unemployment. Econometric analyses have suggested that the declines in labor force participation of the elderly during the last two decades had little effect on the unemployment rate, merely altering the macroeconomic scale of the economy and producing the same effects as deleting from the labor force workers whose names begin with a given letter of the alphabet.[70] In fact, it can be argued that the high cost of social welfare benefits necessary to support the "young-old" in retirement create a dead weight on the economy which makes the nation less competitive and ultimately costs jobs. The older workers of the future will be a much better educated group than those of the past, with skills badly needed in the economy.

Because of the new "baby bust," there will be fewer young workers over the next several decades. Increased energy prices have affected productivity, slowing and even reversing the substitution of energy for labor in producing goods and services. Investments of labor and capital are needed to modernize industry and develop more energy-efficient factories, transportation, and housing. For our economy to resuscitate itself, a shift from consumption to investment will be needed for some decades to come—and, ultimately, increasingly early retirement represents choosing consumption over investment.

Demographic change will add to the burden of supporting the aged. Economic reality is that one generation supports another in retirement, no matter what labels we put on our income maintenance programs. This burden will be exacerbated by the lower rate of real economic growth likely during the 1980s.

Reasons for retirement are somewhat elusive to researchers. Survey respondents frequently say they retired because of "poor health," but this is often a face-saving response. Many older people do look forward to retirement, particularly those in boring jobs.* However, many find themselves bored and isolated once they retire. As labor force participation increases in the rest of society, the workplace becomes more central for socialization and for the feeling of being useful. With more women working in offices and on an equal basis with men, office social life becomes less distinct in quality from off-the-job interaction; and since more of the adult population is working, retired adults have fewer people to interact with apart from one another. These trends are reflected in the media—the office family has become a staple of television situation comedies. Work provides "a set of benefits that are part of the complex social life called Job—a cultural support system . . . Job is the new neighborhood."[71]

All these factors suggest that a new look will need to be taken at retirement policies. The effects of age discrimination legislation and the ban on mandatory retirement at 65 enacted in the mid-seventies are not yet clear, though only a small minority—12 percent—of near-retirement workers in 1981 thought it would have any effect on their own retirement plans.[72] Economic incentives, however, are probably of greater influence. W. Kip Viscusi,[73] in a time-series analysis of labor force participation rates, found that the increasing level of Social Security benefits available at age 65, combined with the severe limitations on earnings without loss of benefits, was a

---

* Although almost half of retirees in the 1981 Harris/NCOA survey said they did not.

major factor in the decline of labor force participation by the elderly.

The treatment of retirement at different ages under Social Security rules is especially significant. Social Security has provided incentives for earlier retirement and discouraged postponing it past the "normal" age of 65. The early retirement penalty is a 6.7 percent benefit reduction for each year by which retirement is moved up from age 65. At 62, for example, one can retire on a grant reduced by 20 percent. The bonus for retiring after 65 is now a 3 percent benefit increase for each year retirement is delayed (it was only 1 percent before 1982). It has been estimated that the early retirement penalty does not make up for the increased number of years the benefit will be drawn, nor does the late retirement bonus make up for the reduced length of retirement.[74] Thus the pension returns are greatest the earlier one retires, and late retirees subsidize early ones. It has been projected[75] that increasing the early retirement penalty to 8 percent a year and the late retirement bonus to 5 percent would substantially increase employment of older workers.

Private pensions offer an even clearer incentive to early retirement than does Social Security. In the 1960s and early 1970s, the proportion of companies allowing early retirement increased, reaching 94 percent by 1974. And among those plans with early retirement provisions, the rules were often liberalized. Previously, many plans required that benefits be actuarially reduced for early retirees. Many companies have dropped these requirements, so that early retirees could expect a greater lifetime benefit than those retiring at 65.

The number of plans providing for early retirement without actuarial reduction increased especially quickly during the early 1970s. A Bankers Trust Company study found that between 1969 and 1974, the proportion of single-employer pension plans requiring full reduction for retirement at the earliest date possible declined from about half to less than 15 percent.[76]

"My Helmet Now Shall Be a Hive for Bees"

Among multiemployer plans, another study showed that the proportion of employees in plans providing for early retirement went from 23 percent in 1960 to 82 percent in 1973.[77] Traditionally, early retirement also required the employer's approval; this was true of three-fifths of plans in the mid-fifties and of half as recently as 1971. In 1974, however, fewer than 10 percent of plans included this requirement.[78]

These early retirement issues concern more than just a marginal couple of years before age 65. Many plans now allow retirement with a full pension at age 55, providing enough years of service were worked. The cause and effect relationship between such provisions and early retirement is clear. In firms with actuarially reduced benefits in 1970, 5 percent of all retirements were early. In firms with less than full actuarial reductions, early retirements represented 30 percent of the total.[79]

In many respects, private pensions exaggerate the division of the work force into an advantaged and disadvantaged sector.[80] While the white-versus-blue-collar distinction is still thought of as the basic categorization of the working world, the division we describe here cuts somewhat differently. The early retirement story repeats the distinctions we found earlier in the receipt of pensions. The advantage tends to be with employees of the large corporations with "command positions" in the economy; with stable workers in stable companies; with employees of manufacturing firms; with technicians, professionals, and managers; with union members; and with men and whites. In effect, what happens is that those without the continuous covered service in one company necessary for early retirement work longer to make retirement possible for others at age 55. Often, the employee is able to take a second job and still collect his pension: in such cases the pension system is not even being used for retirement income. This is particularly common with retired government workers, who can sometimes boost their income to remarkable heights or even qualify for a second pension. It is not unknown for retired police supervisors in large cities to take a second job covered under another pension system, sometimes for another city department, and receive combined compensation much in excess of the mayor's.

Federal jobholders can arrange particularly interesting variations on this theme. They are not part of the Social Security system, and their pensions are calculated to provide a full retirement income at 55. With several years at a second job, they are often able to qualify for a Social Security pension as well. Retirement from the military can take place after 20 years, even before age 40, and retired military have excellent opportunities for pyramiding pensions and salaries, including second government jobs.

In the context of concern about future functioning of the Social Security system, the retirement age issue came to much greater public attention in the early 1980s than ever previously. The problem of coping with the demographic bulge in the 21st century was highlighted in the reports of several advisory committees and study groups, notably including the President's Commission on Pension Policy. The recommendation to shift standard retirement age to 68 on a phased basis by the early 21st century was made in several of the studies of the problem.

The proposed shift to "standard" retirement age of 68 has usually assumed that Social Security rules would be like the current ones, but with all ages moved back for three years. Thus "early retirement" would be possible, with a reduced benefit, at 65 instead of 62. This is a much more severe shift than the increase in the early-retirement penalty and late-retirement bonus proposed above, since not even reduced benefits would be available before 65. A change in standard retirement age under Social Security may become necessary, although we should look first to those private and public employee programs which now provide retirement for an advantaged group at 55 or 60. But if such changes are considered in the basic Social Security entitlement, it is important that they be backstopped by need-tested and disability-tested programs to provide for those who have no realistic choice of working in their mid-sixties.

Many who retire early or at age 65 do so because they are no longer able to work. Some have withdrawn from the labor force before they were eligible for any benefits. In 1981, 37 percent of retirees said they had been forced to retire, and 46 percent said they had not looked forward to stopping work. Forced retirement had been most typical among low-income retirees—45 percent—and a majority among retired blacks had retired involuntarily. Two-thirds of involuntary retirees said they had been forced into retirement by disability or poor health.[81]

There will always be many people unable to work until age 68 with undiminished responsibility. In 1981, 72 percent of workers nearing 65 felt that they would not put off retirement to 68 even if this were to mean a much larger pension.[82] For those who really must stop working before 65, or even before 62, safety nets are needed. The Social Security disability program has served this purpose for many people in the past, when age and skills in relation to jobs actually available were taken into account. But the Reagan administration has moved aggressively toward a more restrictive eligibility procedure both in the Social Security (Title II) and Supplemental Security Income disability programs. Eligibility considerations have been limited much more strictly to medical factors. Many older beneficiaries have been removed from the rolls, based on a belief that they had the physical capacity for some type of gainful activity, without regard to whether work suited to their impairments was actually available. Beneficiaries who are sophisticated or who have the help of knowledgeable family or friends have often been able to get these determinations reversed through appeals, but not all those affected know how to do so effectively.

If Social Security policies on retirement age are changed without changing private pensions, we'll see further movement to a two-class retirement system; and if they are changed without the proper backstopping from disability insurance, Supplementary Security Income, and employment programs, we'll see increasing unemployment and poverty among older workers. What is needed are policies which encourage later retirement for those who are able to work and for whom work is still rewarding, while providing adequately for those who must retire earlier. To do this without unreasonably burdensome increases in total resources will require substantial rethinking of current policies in a number of areas.

Reorganizing Work

The problem of retirement age poses the age-old problem of creating incentives for desired behavior, without unfairly hurting those for whom the desired behavior is simply not an option. Retirement behavior responds strongly to the economic incentives built into pension plans. The Age Discrimination in Employment amendments, moving mandated retirement from 65 to 70, have had relatively little upward effect on average retirement age, while early retirement provisions of Social Security, private and public employee pensions have had considerable downward effect.

As we've seen, many workers at or nearing 65 have difficulty keeping up with the rigors of the full working week and with undiminished responsibilities—especially those who have done manual and/or repetitive work for many years. As with living arrangements, the ideal preferred by many older people is something in between the extremes which are usually available. Remarkably, an overwhelming majority of workers nearing 65 in 1981—79 percent—said they would prefer to continue part-time paid work if possible when they retire, rather than stop working completely. This is a far higher percentage than actually continue to work under present conditions. Three-quarters of workers under 55, and 73 percent of those over 65, say the same. An even greater proportion of low-income workers—84 percent—and of blacks feel this way. And 84 percent of workers nearing retirement feel that greater availability of part-time work would be helpful to them personally.[83]

Potentially, a system of staged retirement could be of great benefit both to older workers and to those of the younger generation who must pay for their retirement. Again, European models are available. In such countries as France, England, and the Netherlands, "gliding out" plans permit a gradual shift to a part-time schedule for older workers.

Other ways of creating flexibility for older workers include jobsharing, allowing some work to be done at home, and more flexible working hours—for example, freedom to set one's own work schedule as long as 70 hours every two weeks are worked. Workers near retirement in the Harris 1981 sample felt these three approaches would be personally helpful to them by, respectively, margins of 73–24, 77–20, and 58–37. By contrast, greater availability of full-time jobs and of a four-day work week were not seen as personally helpful by the majority. The proportion of workers who feel they would want to retire gradually rather than working full time until they retire—37 percent—is less than the proportion who would like to work part-time after retirement. It is striking, however, that almost two-fifths would have wished to retire gradually, an option which is seldom available.

With phased retirement plans, unlike other "grand plans" for reform of retirement systems, nothing stands in the way of leadership by individual corporations. A more flexible approach to employment and a greater acceptance of part-time roles for career employees would also benefit other members of the work force, notably those with child care responsibilities. In addition to "gliding out," what is needed is a departure from the assumption of lockstep upward progression in responsibility until final placement and then retirement. Here we could learn from Japan, where "retired" corporate employees frequently go back to work in positions of lesser responsibility within the same company, or take jobs elsewhere. An old German proverb says *"Rast ich, so rost ich"*—"When I rest, I rust." Many older people feel the same way, but are tired or just bored with the nine-to-five grind, or feel they can't keep up the pace. It's interesting to note that the majority of workers who would like part-time work after retirement would prefer a different kind of work, though the desire for change decreases substantially as retirement is neared. Retirement is a drastic change, at a time in life when the ability or desire to make drastic readjustments may have declined. Seventy percent of 1981 retirees in the 1981 Harris sample said they missed the people at work, 55 percent the feeling of being useful, 48 percent things happening around them, 48 percent the respect of others, and 44 percent having a fixed schedule every day.

But as with living arrangements, older people are usually presented with an all-or-nothing choice. Very few employers permit a shift to part-time work, or a phased shift to less demanding responsibilities—although many private and public employers might find such plans helpful in controlling pension costs as well as enhancing life for older workers.

Under contemporary conditions, the neighborhood and the family cannot always provide the arena for social participation that they did in the past, while the job has become more important. More flexible approaches to work participation will be important in the future, if we are to avoid wasting older workers' talents and, at ever more burdensome cost, supporting a higher and higher proportion of the population in retirement.

6

The Growth of the
Aging-Welfare State
and the Two Worlds
of Aging

WE HAVE ENTERED an era of conflicting pressures: increasing reliance on government by the elderly and a reaction against social spending in a period of economic stagnation. During the 1970s, the cost of maintaining and improving benefits to the aged escalated, putting the squeeze on the entire national budget. Wholesale budget cutting spread in the 1980s. Though other constituencies bore the brunt of the cuts, benefits for the aged represented a major part of the growth in government spending to which this was a reaction. As the population ages, social welfare programs benefiting the aged have matured and past commitments are coming due, so that social welfare is increasingly directed toward the aged. Thus in two senses we have an "aging-welfare state."

The Growth of Federal Expenditures

The increased cost of Social Security has received the most attention. Both the Social Security tax rate and the maximum wage base to which it applies have jumped. For workers whose salary exceeded the maximum wage base, employer-employee contributions increased from $926 each to $1,975 each between 1977 and 1981. By 1987, they will reach $3,046. A look at a table of maximum Social Security tax indicates graphically why the costs of aging-welfare received so little attention in past years and so much recently (see table 6-1). Between the late forties and the late eighties, the tab will have increased more than a hundredfold!

The rising costs reflect the increasing ratio of retirees to contributors, which went from 2 in 1945 and 12 in 1955 to 31 in 1980.[1] They also reflect the fact that the average benefit, particularly during the 1970s, has grown faster than the income of the average worker. The average benefit for a retired worker was $83.92 in 1965, $118.10 in 1970, and $341.41 in 1980;[2] thus it nearly tripled during the seventies. These increases are particularly striking since the figures include an increasing proportion of early retirees who accepted reduced benefits.

Interestingly, the big increases in Social Security benefits took place under the Nixon administration. After growth by only 13 percent between 1960 and 1965, and little more in the late sixties, a 15 percent flat benefit increase in 1970 was followed by a 10 percent increase in 1971 and a 20 percent increase in 1972. In 1972, also, indexing of benefits to the Consumer Price Index was enacted. The law's formulas created an anomaly with potential effects understood by very few of the lawmakers at the time.[3] It had the effect of "double-indexing"

TABLE 6-1

Social Security Maximum Tax

Year	Maximum Contribution	Year	Maximum Contribution
1937–49	$ 30	1972	$ 468
1950	45	1973	632
1951–53	54	1974	772
1954	72	1975	825
1955–56	84	1976	895
1957–58	95	1977	926
1959	120	1978	1,071
1960–61	144	1979	1,404
1962	150	1980	1,588
1963–65	174	1981	1,975
1966	277	1982	2,131
1967	290	1983	2,271
1968	343	1984	2,412
1969–70	374	1985	2,686
1971	406	1986	2,874
		1987	3,046

SOURCE: Research Institute of America, presented in James Jorgensen, *The Graying of America: Retirement and Why You Can't Afford It* (New York: McGraw-Hill, 1980), p. 174.

retirement benefits both to the Consumer Price Index *and* to rising pre-retirement wages on which benefits were calculated. The formula was highly sensitive to the rate of inflation. Because the inflation rate in the mid-seventies was much higher than expected in 1972, real benefits increased during the mid-seventies faster than had been anticipated, until the formula was finally adjusted in 1977.[4] The increases of this period built up the base on which later cost-of-living increases were calculated. Then during the late seventies, industrial productivity declined and the Consumer Price Index, which had previously lagged average wage increases for workers, grew faster than wages. Again, retirees improved their position relative to that of the employed, and program costs escalated.

But Social Security is only part of the problem. Costs of public employee pensions, health care, and other benefits have also escalated. Over only a few years, these total costs have become perhaps the most crucial problem of domestic social policy.

By a mid-1981 Office of Management and Budget (OMB) estimate, federal spending for the elderly was $144 billion for fiscal year 1980, $168 billion for fiscal 1981, and $191 billion for fiscal 1982.[5] The fiscal year 1982 figure constituted 27.4 percent of the total budget of $695 billion. This level of spending was estimated to amount to an average of $7,600 per aged person, or $15,200 per aged couple. Health expenditures alone were estimated at an average of $3,900 per couple.

These levels of expenditure are considerably in excess of the public impression. In a small New York phone survey, estimates of costs of aging programs averaged about 10 percent of the federal budget. The public seems to overestimate the cost of public assistance for the non-aged, and underestimate the cost of benefits for the aged. There is also some reason to think the public might prefer to allocate a higher percentage of social spending to children and the poor than actually goes to them.[6]

Government budgets shift from year to year; however, table 6-2 gives a sense of the scope of benefits going to the aged. A full account of federal spending on the aged and for retirement programs would produce even larger estimates. Many retirement benefits, for example, go to persons under 65. Federal employee retirement and disability expenditures are budgeted at $19.9 billion in the income security part of the budget for civilian employees, and at an additional $15.6 billion in the defense part of the budget for military pensions. In addition, many expenditures are difficult to break out by age. All together, benefits to persons over 65 and for retirement programs probably make up for about a third of the federal budget. And none of this accounts for the fast-growing tax expenditures (see appendix, table 16).

A look at these budget breakdowns shows first that the vast bulk of federal spending on the aged is in non-means-tested

The Growth of Federal Expenditures

TABLE 6-2
Federal Outlays Benefiting the Elderly
(Millions of Dollars)

Program	Actual FY80	Projected FY82
Administration on Aging	679	651
Volunteers Programs	72	84
National Institute on Aging	58	77
Employment Programs	238	279
Medicare	29,331	39,230
Medicaid	4,658	5,756
Other Federal Health Programs	2,030	2,347
Social Security	81,224	111,042
Other Retired, Disabled, and Survivors Benefits (includes Railroad Retirement)	14,477	17,586
Supplemental Security Income	2,274	2,926
Veterans Compensation and Pensions	3,257	4,255
Subsidized Public Housing	2,255	3,359
Elderly Housing Loans	723	741
Food Stamps	483	565
Social Services (Title XX)	489	394
Energy Assistance	272	225
Other	1,025	1,156
Total	143,545	190,673

SOURCE: Testimony by David Stockman, Director of the Office of Management and Budget, before the House Select Committee on Aging, April 6, 1981.

programs. In fact, only about a tenth of the total is, at least in theory, means-tested. (As we've seen, even programs which are theoretically means-tested often don't work out that way.) Second, most of the programs which *are* means-tested were disproportionately cut in real terms under Reagan—the Title XX social services program, for example, was a major victim. The large non-means-tested benefits did relatively well under the Reagan budgets, compared to programs for poor children, adults, and elderly; thus in the proposed fiscal year 1983 budget, an even higher proportion of all social spending than previously was directed to the elderly, and of this an even higher percentage than before was non-means-tested.

By OMB estimate, the percentage of the federal budget going to the aged was projected to increase from 24.9 in 1980 to 27.4

in 1982[7] and 28 percent or more in 1983, while expenditures for children and the nonelderly poor declined sharply. If the ratio of public expenditures per capita for the elderly and for youth was 3 to 1 in 1975,[8] it probably reached 4 to 1 by 1982.

Spending for the elderly has been affected by trends with multiplicative effects: demographic developments, improvements in benefit levels, increased reliance on and take-up of benefits. As financial pressures increase, competition between the elderly (along with their service providers) and other groups has increased. Social Security and Medicare have remained so popular that they have been hard to cut, despite the enormous pressures created by tax cuts, increased defense spending, and record deficits. Reagan discovered this in 1981, when the administration had to beat a disorderly retreat from proposals for immediate benefit reductions in Social Security, and again in 1982 when he embraced and then quickly backed off from a Republican budget proposal incorporating a $40 billion saving in Social Security. But the programs which have been a lifeline for the poor elderly—Title XX social services funding which provided much home care, food stamps, energy assistance, Medicaid, nutrition programs—were slashed.

The elderly constituency is politically potent when it comes to issues that affect them all, but has often been less so on true "safety net" programs which constitute the floor under the economic well-being of the aged and their access to services. This is because the interests of differently situated older people are divergent. The concerns of the younger and more comfortably-off aged, who vote, organize, and make themselves heard, do not necessarily coincide with those of the aged in greatest need. The former are most often concerned with the maintenance of pre-retirement middle-class standards of living, tax benefits, and "life-enhancing" programs. The latter need basic survival aid. Social Security and Medicare, especially, are prime concerns of the organized, middle-class elderly constituency, while Supplementary Security Income, Medicaid, Food

Stamps, and the like are not comparable priorities for them. The interplay of interests in the political marketplace can't be counted on to balance the needs.

The Frail and the Frisky Elderly

As we've seen, the subliminal assumption that the aged are homogeneous, with severe deprivation and ill health typical, distorts understanding and shaping of policies. As long as a policy benefits people who are old, it's assumed that it is helping the deprived—just who benefits is not further scrutinized. But the interests of the two increasingly unequal worlds of aging differ. The better-off elderly tend to be young-old (65–74), married, in good health, with assets and income from private pensions and investments, and/or white. The world of the worst-off elderly is quite different. They tend to be old-old, in poor health with chronic impairments, widowed, isolated, living only on Social Security or SSI, and/or nonwhite. And, disproportionately, the world of the worst-off aged is a woman's world.

As we have shown, these characteristics tend to cluster in patterns of "multiple jeopardy": for example, poor health is associated with being nonwhite, with having lower income, with very advanced age, with nonmarried status, and so on. Thus in the 1981 Harris survey, bad health was a very serious problem for 12 percent of high-income elderly and 31 percent of those with the lowest incomes; for 48 percent of Hispanics, 35 percent of blacks, and 18 percent of whites; for 14 percent of those with private pension coverage, and 25 percent of those without. Sixty-three percent of blacks, versus 41 percent of white elderly, rated their health as fair or poor. Chapter 5 showed how these differentials in self-perceived health by income level and race are matched by a similar distribution of objective indicators of chronic illness and impairment.

Similarly, economic deprivation is concentrated among "multiple jeopardy" groups—those over 75, the single and widowed, women, nonwhites, and especially those with several of these characteristics. These patterns appear both in objective indicators of poverty (see chapter 2) and in indicators of self-perceived financial distress. When asked whether "not having enough money to live on" was a personal problem, 62 percent of white elderly chose the "hardly a problem at all" response. For blacks and Hispanics, the most common response (42 and 52 percent, respectively) was that this was a "very serious" problem.

Eighty percent of black elderly and 46 percent of whites felt they couldn't make ends meet, or just about managed to get by. At the other end of the scale, 20 percent of white elderly and 25 percent of private pension holders, versus 5 percent of blacks and 13 percent of non-pension-holders, felt they could buy pretty much whatever they wanted.

Statistics on income inequality actually understate the racial differences in the economic well-being of the aged. Elderly who do not have adequate income are also unlikely to have a paid-for home or to have savings available to spend. Black elderly, with 54 percent of mean white income in 1980, had a 44 percent chance of having a paid-off home, as compared with a 70 percent chance for white elderly. Twenty-seven percent of low-income elderly, versus 5 percent of high-income elderly, were renters. And 28 percent of those with household income under $5,000, versus only 1 percent of those at $20,000 or more, volunteered that they had no savings at all.[9]

Six percent of those with private pension coverage said they had no savings, versus 17 percent of those without such coverage. Thirty-eight percent of the black elderly and only 9 percent of whites were without savings. Only 4 percent of the low-income elderly, and 61 percent at $20,000 or over, had investments other than savings. Investments were owned by whites eight times as often as by blacks, and twelve times as often as by Hispanics.

Those with higher incomes, whites, men, and those with pension coverage are thus more likely to have savings, but they are less likely to be spending from savings. Seventy-five percent of elderly with incomes over $20,000, versus 29 percent of those under $5,000, had not spent any of their savings in the past year. Whites were twice as likely as nonwhites to have kept their savings untouched.

The worst-off elderly are in no position to avail themselves of many of the public benefits available to the well-off elderly. They are much less likely to benefit from tax subsidies on private pension funds, Keogh plans, or individual retirement accounts, or from the $125,000 exemption from capital gains taxation on a sale of a principal residence after age 55. A tax deduction is worth a great deal to an elderly person in a high income bracket, nothing at all to an elderly person who does not even earn enough to pay taxes, or who does not itemize deductions. The increasing importance of tax-related benefits like IRA's will do little for the truly needy.

Retirement means different things in the two worlds. In the 1981 Harris survey, those with higher incomes and private pension coverage usually had looked forward to retirement, while almost two-thirds of the low income aged had not. Since the lower-income aged had typically retired from less skilled and more onerous jobs, the difference is probably the result of financial worries, not intrinsic satisfactions of the job. The majority of the poor aged only retired when they were forced to, either by the employer or by poor health, while more than two-thirds of higher-income elderly retired by choice. Blacks and those with low educations were less likely to retire by choice. And when they did retire, poorer, nonwhite, and less educated aged were less likely to have prepared themselves. The Harris questionnaire identified a number of steps in preparation for retirement, ranging from developing hobbies and leisure-time activities to being sure medical care would be available. In every area, nonwhites and those with lower education and income were less prepared.[10]

The dramatic increases in old-age and retirement programs during the 1960s and 1970s improved the average living standard of the elderly, relative to that of the nonelderly. They did so, however, in a scattershot fashion, leaving many behind. Public policies do not establish a reasonable minimum base of adequacy, despite the massive increase in spending. This is especially true for the "multiple jeopardy" groups. While 8 percent of white elderly men lived in poverty in 1977, 41 percent of black women, and two-thirds of black women living alone, were below the poverty line (see chapter 2).

The principle of giving the truly needy priority in public benefits has been much espoused lately, particularly by conservatives concerned with the scope of government spending. In aging policy, however, we have moved no closer to this goal—in fact, recent trends have been away from it.

In the past, the smaller proportion of aged, the greater availability of informal aid, and economic and population growth made it possible to bypass some of the difficult choices, and to "spread the wealth around" generously, creating an easy consensus in which everyone had something to gain. Conditions in the eighties and beyond make choices more stark. It will become apparent that one person's gain is another's cost. In this "zero-sum society," explicit equity decisions must be faced in public policies.[11] Doing so for old-age programs will require rethinking the distributional consequences of aging-welfare.

The massive increase in aid to the aged, and the relative improvement of the economic status of the aged as a group in comparison with the non-aged, might be taken to suggest that the problem of deprivation among the aged has largely been solved. But what would be fairer to say is that the *total* flow of resources, through organized programs, from the working to the older generation is now probably sufficient or nearly so.

Women

Progress has been made: witness the improved poverty rates. The aged *as a group* are no longer a deprived class. But there are still too many left in the cold—though the resources are sufficient, if distributed somewhat differently, easily to provide a reasonable minimum level of decency.

Women

Women and particularly widows predominate among the worst-off aged. In 1976, 28 percent of elderly married couples and 21 percent of unmarried aged men, but only 12 percent of elderly nonmarried women, had income from private pensions. Among those in their immediate postretirement years (65–67), unmarried women had a median income of $3,730 compared with $9,710 for couples, and 72 percent of the elderly poor were unmarried women.[12]

As we have seen, older women are much more likely than men to live alone and to need long-term health care. Public assistance for the aged—Supplementary Security Income—is more than twice as likely to be used by elderly women as by men, 9 versus 4 percent in the Harris 1981 survey. Fifty-three percent of women, versus 45 percent of men, said they were unable to make ends meet or just about managed to get by. Fourteen percent, versus 9 percent of men, had no savings. Twenty-five percent, versus 42 percent of men, received private or public-employee pension income.

Many private plans in the past made no provision for surviving spouses. ERISA required that participants be offered an optional "joint and survivor" benefit, usually paying 50 percent of the worker's pension to the surviving spouse. The cost of this election must be paid through a lowered basic benefit amount, and it is not always chosen. Often, still, the widow gets nothing.

income

Social Security does not work to the advantage of the working married woman. The rules implicitly consider the non-working wife to be the norm. A working woman is entitled to either the pension based on her husband's earning record, generally 50 percent of the husband's benefit, or that based on her own—not to any combination of both. If, as is typical, she earned less than he did, she usually finds her work has netted her little or nothing. A working couple will receive significantly less in total benefits than a couple with the same pre-retirement income, all received by the husband.[13] The widow of the two-income marriage may well receive as little as half the benefit of the widow of the equivalent one-income marriage.

Program Models and Policy Choices

In the evolution of social welfare for the aged, benefits were added piecemeal in response to perceived needs and the pressures of advocacy groups. The various major benefits reflect different program design and eligibility principles, which shape who gains from them and who pays for them.

Social Security reflects a hybrid of return-on-contributions and adequacy principles, and there appears to be substantial public support for both concepts. If a strict insurance concept were followed, it would mean that the recipient would get back the actuarial equivalent of his own contributions, with interest. Since the program is pay-as-you-go, there's no way to know, except by arbitrary assumptions, what an individual's contributions would have earned. But much more important, the preponderance of public sentiment seems to be that adequacy should be considered, rather than following a rigid insurance model. There's also a consensus that higher contributors should get higher grants. Social Security, by replacing higher percentages of the lower salaries, is a compromise.

Program Models and Policy Choices

The distributional issues in Social Security benefits and financing have been much debated since the program's early days.[14] Roosevelt parted company from the leading advocates of old age pensions, such as Abraham Epstein, Isaac Rubinow, and Francis Townsend, on the issue of financing. Epstein and other reformers argued for subsidizing the Social Security funds with general tax revenues in order to redistribute resources. Roosevelt's advisers elected a regressive payroll tax instead; this tends to cancel out the progressive character of income taxation. It produces, in combination with income tax loopholes, a total tax system which is much less progressive than income tax tables suggest. Recent wage base increases have shifted somewhat more of the burden to the middle class. However, the lack of progressivity is a larger issue when the Social Security tax itself is larger. Roosevelt also made the fateful decision to design the system on a pay-as-you-go basis (although in the Depression, with demand at a low ebb in the economy, any other choice was probabaly infeasible).

Supplemental Security Income (SSI) is the successor to Aid to the Aged, Blind and Disabled, providing public assistance on a straightforward means-tested basis. Considering that SSI is the one program that defines the societally established "floor" on economic well-being for the aged, it accounts for a surprisingly small proportion of total federal expenditures on aging—about 1.5 percent. SSI provides what amounts to a survival level of support, typically below the poverty line.

The two major health programs that help the aged provide overlapping services but are organized on diametrically opposed models. The model for Medicare is a social insurance, non-means-tested one. Benefits are available irrespective of financial need to persons eligible for Social Security pensions. Insurance for hospital stays and certain related services is available without charge, and supplementary insurance for physician bills and several other medical services can be bought on a subsidized basis.

153

Most but not all elderly are eligible; those missing out on coverage also tend to have few other resources. Nineteen percent of Hispanic elderly, versus 8 percent of blacks and 4 percent of whites, are uncovered by Medicare or any other health insurance; this is true of 7 percent of low income elderly and 1 percent of those with household income above $10,000.[15]

For the majority who do have Medicare coverage, the "equal" benefits are unequal in practice. The better-off aged are more sophisticated in seeking out medical care, tend to live in areas where the supply of medical care is greatest, face fewer transportation barriers, and in other ways find it easier to utilize their Medicare benefits. Most important, Medicare pays for only part of medical costs incurred. Deductibles (fixed amounts which must be paid each year before the supplementary benefits are provided, and for each hospital stay) and coinsurance (a percentage of the cost of medical services, and of hospital care beyond an allowed number of days) must be paid by the patient. These charges, in amounts unrelated to the patient's income, are imposed to restrain the use of services. But they are much more of a disincentive to low-income than high-income elderly.

In addition, higher-income elderly typically purchase private insurance tailored to supplement Medicare and to pick up the costs which it does not cover; these insurance policies are widely marketed. In 1981, half the high-income elderly had Blue Cross/Blue Shield, compared with 31 percent of low-income elderly. Forty-eight percent of high-income elderly versus 19 percent of low-income elderly had other private insurance. Only 8 percent of Hispanic elderly had Blue Cross/Blue Shield, compared with an overall 46 percent of whites.[16]

The result of these differences has been greater use of Medicare by high-income elderly and by whites, even though low-income elderly and nonwhites suffer from poorer health. In 1968, elderly with incomes over $15,000 received reimbursements more than twice as great as those received on average by those with incomes under $5,000.[17] Higher income people used more services and also saw providers who charged higher rates. The deductible appeared to be a major deterrent: 55 percent of the high-income elderly, versus 43 percent of those with low income, spent enough of their own money (or that of an insurance firm) to cover the deductible and be eligible for Medicare reimbursement.

Another study, using data from 12,000 elderly surveyed in the 1968 Health Interview Survey of the National Center for Health Statistics, compared Medicare utilization by high-income and low-income elderly with comparable health status. Higher income elderly in poor health averaged 17 reimbursed physician visits annually, versus 12 for lower-income elderly in poor health. They also were hospitalized almost half again as often.[18]

Similar differences existed by race. In 1969, whites averaged 40 percent more reimbursement than nonwhites—largely because fewer nonwhites exceeded the deductible under the supplementary part of the program.

The gap in Medicare utilization by race appears to have narrowed somewhat, though not disappeared, during the seventies.[19] However, in the early eighties the level of cost sharing by the patient has been increased substantially, with every indication of a trend to further increases. We may well find ourselves with a utilization pattern quite similar to that of the late sixties, as a result of continuing and increasing reliance on cost sharing as a cost-control measure.

In the 1981 Harris data, it was still apparent that real barriers still exist to using medical services, and taking advantage of Medicare, on the part of low-income aged. About 10 percent of low-income elderly, versus about 1 percent of high-income elderly, said they had not seen a doctor for a health problem for which they felt they should, because it was too expensive. Low-income elderly were also much more likely to report that they hadn't seen a doctor because it was hard to get to his office or hospital, because waits were too long, or because they didn't have a doctor.[20]

Most official proposals for controlling the mushrooming costs of Medicare have depended, in various ways, on increasing coinsurance and deductibles. For example, a plan proposed by the Reagan administration early in 1982 would dramatically increase copayments for hospital care. Under present law the second through sixtieth days of hospitalization are paid in full by Medicare, after which charges beginning at 10 percent are imposed. Under the proposed plan, Medicare patients would be charged $26 for each day of hospitalization after the first, up to a ceiling of $2,500, after which a catastrophic cost provision would take over.*

Another plan, in the President's Fiscal Year 1983 budget proposal, would add copayments to the limited home health benefit which Medicare provides. Perhaps because this service now lacks copayments, it has been the one service which has been used *more* by nonwhites than by whites;[21] this pattern would probably change if co-insurance were imposed.

Medicaid has a very different history from Medicare. Growing out of the public assistance programs under the Social Security Act, its benefits have always been means-tested. As the analysis of long-term care indicated, however, income tests have rather different distributional consequences for high-cost "total" and often permanent care than they have for other services. We've seen that utilization of long-term care under Medicaid is considerably less for nonwhites than whites, and probably is skewed by social class as well.

Many of the equity problems in these health programs involve their publicly financed but privately operated design, and

* Another major administration proposal for Medicare cost control—holding permissible Medicare rate increases below cost increases—shifts costs to other patients, since hospitals raise their Blue Cross and self-pay rates to make up the difference.

Program Models and Policy Choices

the failure to confront the issues of rationing and gatekeeping explicitly. As medical sociologist David Mechanic has commented: "No system of care in the world is willing to provide as much care as people will use, and all such systems develop mechanisms that ration . . . services."[22] When policies do not explicitly confront this issue, the rationing mechanisms which emerge are likely to favor those who are better able to negotiate the system and to "leverage" public resources with their own.

Nursing homes illustrate this theme. Means testing is further vitiated by the difficulty in enforcing transfer of assets provisions:

My children, God bless them, they do the best they can. Of course, I don't see them that often but then, they're busy, they've got their own lives. But they try, they try. For instance, my son, last year he said to me, "Ma, let me take care of your money; then you won't have any money on the record and you'll be eligible for [Medicaid]. So that's what we did. He takes care of everything for me now.[23]

Most of the federal resources which assist the aged are provided through the social insurance, tax deduction, and welfare models we have described. Less important in the total "aging budget" than these open-ended entitlements has been closed-ended funding for programs under which services vary from state to state and locality to locality. The two principal vehicles for such funding have been the Older Americans Act and Title XX of the Social Security Act.

Like Medicaid, Title XX was an outgrowth of the Social Security Act's welfare programs, providing federal reimbursement for a wide range of "social services" to present, past, and potential recipients of public assistance, with broad state discretion.[24] "Potential recipients" have been defined by income ceilings above welfare levels, varying by state and type of service. Senior citizen centers have been one important service to the aged under Title XX. These services have frequently been provided under the principle of "group eligibility," in which age becomes the only qualifying factor for an individual.

Senior centers have created an important opportunity for social interaction, nutrition and counseling for many older people. They have not always reached the more vulnerable, frail, isolated, or poor elderly, however, who may need help with transportation or who are shy and reticent. The other major service typically provided to the elderly under Title XX is home care. Because of its high cost, individual means tests are generally applied for eligibility; thus home care under Title XX is targeted to the relatively poor elderly.

Title XX programs have done much for the elderly in some states, little in others. In California, 62 percent of Title XX funds in 1979 went to providing home care alone, while in other states relatively little of the Title XX allocation goes for services to the aged. Title XX originally provided open-ended federal reimbursement, but the "capping" of the program in the early 1970s limited its ability to provide "hard services" to the aged. With reductions in Title XX funds in the early 1980s, states were forced into Draconian decisions, pitting elderly beneficiaries of home care against children in day care and a myriad of other groups.

Title XX began life with the separation of social services from income maintenance in public assistance. Social services for the poor were to be provided under separate auspices from welfare and without "welfare stigma." The capping, and the broad range of services covered, gave it many of the characteristics of a block grant, though constrained to some extent by federal rules on financial eligibility and other policies. In the Reagan block grant program, the already flexible federal rules were almost entirely eliminated—most notably, financial eligibility standards. It is not yet clear to what extent states will actually take advantage of this flexibility, with fewer dollars available, but the abandonment of most federal standards does give states the option to move away from targeting to the "truly needy" or even the "pretty needy."

Unlike Title XX, the Older Americans Act escaped most of the initial Reagan cuts, and it was not block-granted. This program, however, is also limited in capacity for "hard services," by funding and by a legislative and administrative emphasis on coordinative services. Older Americans Act programs, for the most part, are not means-tested.[25] Carroll Estes[26] has argued that these programs implicitly assume the needs of the aged are similar, lumping together all the elderly with little focus on effects of class, race, sex, and ethnicity. She concludes that "hardship differences among the aged were underplayed in favor of social and recreational programs for which all the aged were eligible. This approach eradicated the visibility of the elderly who were poor, extremely disabled, or ill." Her view is that the emphasis is on life-enhancing services rather than life-support services needed by the aged poor, and that the strategy is designed to meet the needs of the recently deprived elderly and enable them to maintain their middle class life styles, rather than aiding the long-term deprived. Furthermore, she suggests, the emphasis on coordinating rather than directly providing services filters assistance through a corps of professional middlemen who form an "aging establishment."

Problems with the distribution of in-kind benefits are not by any means limited to the United States. In Great Britain, the Royal Commission on the Distribution of Income and Wealth found that in 1975, among one and two person pensioner households in the Family Expenditure Survey, the top 10 percent had an average net income of £31.52 per week and received £8.66 per week in direct and indirect benefits in kind. The bottom 10 percent had an average net income of £12.92 per week and received £5.38 per week in average benefits.[27]

Cui Bono: *Who Benefits from Benefits?*

The overall structure of programs for the aged produces inequities. These result from formal program eligibility rules, differences in the ability to manipulate the system, "creaming" by providers, ethnic and class differences in life span, and ethnic and class differences in the utilization of services, among other factors. The elderly are distinctive among age groups in that the majority of their support comes through governmentally administered and subsidized programs. While available data are limited, it does not appear that this fact has resulted in any less inequality among the aged than exists among the non-aged whose primary support comes through the economy. Income inequality among the aged appears to be, if anything, greater than among the non-aged; Thurow concludes their incomes are much more skewed than those of the rest of the population.[28]

A "status attainment" model of the predictors of income in old age found that despite the change in the sources of income, "the relation of status variables to income remains almost untouched in old age."[29] The socioeconomic factors which predict income in the working years—education and occupational status especially—predict income even better in retirement. Income sources including Social Security, pensions, and continued work function as intervening variables in a process by which the social class system persists into old age. Despite a substantial increase in public benefits between 1955 and 1964, one study found no change in income inequality among the aged in that period. A "Gini index" of inequality among unrelated individuals 65 or over was computed at .416 for 1955, .418 for 1960, and .419 for 1964. For families headed by someone 65 or over the index was .467, .468, and .469 for the three years.[30] This analysis measured income inequality; as we have shown, the distribution of assets is even more unequal.

The well-being of the aged depends on many factors; but there is evidence that to an extent money *can* buy happiness—

or, at least, its absence buys unhappiness. The 1981 Harris survey included a life-satisfaction scale. High income respondents scored 43 percent higher than those with low income; the gap was up from 30 percent in 1974.[31] Data from life-satisfaction scales need to be taken with several grains of salt, but life certainly can be very difficult for the elderly poor.

The consistent pattern in aging policy has been the choice of "strong clients with weak claims" over "weak clients with strong claims."[32] Making changes involves many powerfully vested interests—literally "vested" in the case of pension programs. It involves the prerogatives of powerful institutions and providers, including the "medical-industrial complex" which the editor of the *New England Journal of Medicine* has warned of.[33]

The aggregate flow of resources from the working to the elderly generation, through publicly funded and subsidized programs, is probably now sufficient. What is now necessary is to better target these resources so that a minimum level of economic decency and access to basic services is assured in old age.

7

Where Do We Go from Here?

AS WE HAVE SEEN, realities differ from widely held assumptions as to the characteristics of the aged, their needs, their sources of help, and the effects of the programs that serve them. Making wise choices requires that we move past the myths and misunderstandings.

One myth has been the idea that the extended family plays an unchanged, substantial role in supporting most aged. Both the "unimpaired extended family" and the "isolated nuclear family" models are much too simple. The family in modern society is a complex institution in a complex setting. However, the very real trend toward generational independence which has taken place cannot be ignored. It is important that we be realistic about the limits to family help available for many of the elderly.

Sentimentality on this point could be dangerous. An important lesson can be found in the history of mental hospital deinstitutionalization. The impetus for that movement came, to a considerable degree, from liberal social scientists and reformers.

Institutions and Communities

During the 1960s, social critics increasingly assailed mental hospitals and pressed to curtail them. This, along with cost considerations, helped lead to wholesale reductions in the populations of the institutions. The rejection of mental hospitals, as well as the rediscovery of the family in relation to the aged, were part of broader intellectual currents which elevated informal structures—the community, the ethnic group, the extended family—above formal and bureaucratic ones. Regard for professions and professionals, along with the institutions they controlled, declined, and was replaced in some instances by an unrealistically optimistic faith in the community's ability to absorb and support "problem people."

Reformers acknowledged that a proper policy of "deinstitutionalization" would require creating services in the community to replace those in the large institutions. But there were many barriers to putting those services into place—not only cost but the reluctance of communities to accept former patients and programs for them. Rather than taking responsibility for creating the alternative services, some officials consciously decided that if the patients were pushed out of the institutions, the community would then be forced to absorb them;[1] and reformers tacitly accepted this.

Deinstitutionalization of the mental hospitals was the result of a number of forces. Cost concerns were critical, especially since accreditation agencies and sometimes judges were forcing the mental hospitals to upgrade the low, sometimes abysmal levels of staffing and quality of care they had provided. The

163

new tranquilizers made it possible to stabilize patients' behavior and made them more manageable outside a hospital. The tacit alliance of people with very different agendas—social reformers and budgetary officials—led to rapid and drastic declines in the population of the hospitals.

As actually played out, the process represented in large measure a triumph of sentiment over sense, and cost cutting over caring. In state after state, institutions were emptied out with little in the way of alternative services to transfer the patients to. Many of the older patients were placed in nursing homes, while some of the younger ones became part of the helpless, marginal urban population in single-room welfare hotels or, in some cases, in the ranks of the homeless. The patients were no better off, often worse: by supporting the release of patients prior to the availability of alternative care, social critics accomplished no real reform.

Now, nursing homes in turn are coming under severe budgetary pressures. In many states, certificate-of-need laws have been applied to hold supplies far below demands. Since it seemed that the full demand could not be satisfied by any level of supply within financial reach, since there was concern that nursing homes might be displacing family effort, and since it seemed so difficult to eliminate "inappropriate" use of homes, the issue was often forced by more-or-less arbitrary caps on the further approval of beds. Indeed—as we've seen—long-term care policy has depended far too much on nursing homes. But this time, it is important that the alternative services be put in place first—as in fact has happened in some states. Many patients who now use nursing homes and other organized long-term care services have only limited family supports available, or have already exhausted them. It would be quite unrealistic to expect the family to fill the breach, if the organized services were not available.

Nursing homes do fill an important place in a continuum of care. If sufficient in-home services are available, it will be easier to limit the use of nursing homes to those circumstances where they really are the most appropriate answer. For patients who need constant attention and for those with advanced organic brain syndrome, for example, the nursing home will most often be the best answer. Nursing homes have become extremely unpopular, but it would be unfortunate if a backlash resulted in the unavailability of needed care. It is all too easy for those concerned only with reducing budgets to use faith in the resources of the family to justify policies which would try to force such informal support by withdrawing formal supports.

There are ways to reduce unnecessary use of nursing homes, but they all require alternative spending and careful attention to the issues of assessment and access. When supplies are artificially constrained in the absence of such efforts, serious inequities and other problems result. There's a serious risk that only those who have resources of their own to cover an initial stay, or who have "pull," will be able to get a bed in a decent home, while those who must start off as Medicaid patients end up in the worst homes, are sent far from family to wherever a home is available, or can't get care at all. This isn't a theoretical concern: in 1981, for example, a grand jury found that access to many better homes in New York depended on contributions made by patients' families even though the care itself was paid for by Medicaid.[2] The tighter supply becomes, without controls on access, the more likely these developments come to be, and the harder it becomes to regulate nursing homes in a seller's market.

In these and other ways, it often works out that working-class, minority, and poor families end up carrying greater burdens for their parents' care than do the children of the middle class. When we do not take explicit responsibility for determining access to benefits, in the face of demands greater than supplies, we sweep problems of equity under the rug and allow rationing processes to emerge whose results would be difficult to justify as conscious choices.

Some gerontologists associated in the 1960s with the "unimpaired extended family" position now take a subtly modified stand, suggesting that families carry out their helping role in large part by serving as go-betweens that link the elderly with bureaucratic benefit systems.[3] But not all the elderly have comparable access to such go-betweens. If we develop service systems which are so complex and arcane that the extensive labor of an advocate is necessary in order to get access to them, we can expect the results to be unequal.

The System of Old Age Policy

The aging-welfare system developed incrementally—program by program and benefit by benefit. To do better, we need to replace the program orientation with a policy focus, looking at the total impact of government actions, rules, and inactions. We need to analyze incidence of costs and of benefits, intended and unintended effects. We need to go beyond the explicit eligibility rules of programs to look empirically at how and by whom they are actually utilized. Eligibility rules intersect with informal social organization, cultural and social class differences, and differential access skills and resources to determine how program benefits are reaped.

In such analysis, several motifs recur. First, everything affects everything else. The role of government and other formal systems in care of the aged affects informal social structures such as the family—and vice versa. A corollary to this is "no action without reaction": interventions have side effects, often unanticipated or counterintuitive, bringing new problems in their wake. A pull anywhere on the social web has effects throughout the structure. One author[4] hyperbolized this principle as "all problems are the result of solutions."

Because of these complex interactions, the real consequences of policy choices are not at all obvious. Understanding is further clouded by myths of aging. For example, to the extent it is assumed that all elderly are needy, programs which on their face benefit people who happen to be old escape scrutiny as to just which old people are helped. Given finite resources, it is necessary to examine and choose more critically among alternative means of aiding the aged.

In examining the aging-welfare system, one recurringly encounters incoherence: the pervasive, unnecessary, and confusing complexity of structure and rules. As a result, access to benefits is determined too much by the luck of the draw and by the ability to "use the system." Old-age benefits fail to constitute a reliable "social safety net." We tend to isolate the elderly and "pension them off" from meaningful social interactions. The system fails to provide opportunities to replace the loss of social roles and the chance for participation, productivity, and usefulness to others. Despite its failure to guarantee access to a minimum level of basic resources, it is ferociously, and increasingly, expensive.

Ultimately, the aged will include almost all of us. The policies that transfer resources from particular members of the working-age population to particular members of the aged population involve the distribution of resources among socioeconomic groups—often from the poorer to the richer in terms of lifetime socioeconomic level.

In the 1960s and 1970s, while benefits were expanding, choices could be avoided which now are harder to escape. If we do not expect the system to be all things for all people, the resources presently going to the system could provide a much more secure, decent "social safety net" than they do at present. A criterion of equity would include "vertical equity" between the best-off and worst-off aged, men and women, whites and blacks, the old-old and the young-old. It would also include "horizontal equity"—similar benefits for those similarly situated, as compared with the present role of chance and luck.

It is easier to identify what's wrong with the system, and to suggest directions and principles for reform, than it is to specify a detailed reform program. Choices in old-age policy really represent decisions as to who will benefit and who will pay. A balance between universal and need-tested benefits is necessary. People at almost all economic levels need help in old age, if only because of the difficulty we all have in deferring gratification to meet future needs and the unpredictable vicissitudes of age. Services restricted to the poor tend to become poor services. Further, all reforms create new problems.

Nevertheless, principles for improvements can be suggested. The principal themes are: guaranteeing a more adequate minimum level of economic well-being and access to services; placing some limits on the proliferation of tax subsidies and other benefits which principally aid the best-advantaged; improving public benefits rather than "privatizing" them; making existing privately run systems such as private pensions fairer; providing alternatives to institutional care; maintaining productive participation by the elderly in the society, including the workplace, as long as feasible; encouraging informal support systems; and providing the conditions—for example, through age-concentrated housing—for the aged to replace lost roles and relationships with peer networks.

A Many-Splintered Thing: The Long-Term Care System

A more coherent, rational long-term care system is badly needed. Demographic pressures on long-term care will be greater than those on pension systems in the next several decades, because the very old population at greatest risk will be increasing much faster than the total number of elderly. As this and other pressures increase, it will become all the more important that we get our act together.

A Many-Splintered Thing

As we've seen, the long-term care system has resisted many attempted reforms, through its sheer complexity and the strength of vested interests. Nevertheless, change is needed; sustained and intelligent effort over time can produce important results, and the chance of success will be greatest if we bear in mind the basic structural problems of the existing system.

One key to reform is to treat long-term care as, literally, a system. As it stands, access to almost every form of long-term care involves different procedures and organizations. Planning, policy-setting, assessment, and referral for various forms of long-term care need to be administratively integrated. This would make more rational planning possible, and would remove at least one set of barriers to the development of systems which integrate assessment and placement for all forms of long-term care. Long-term care, under Medicaid and Title XX, has been highly decentralized, and a host of variations among different states exist which require evaluation. A number of federally funded experiments are also in progress which are testing ways to "channel" patients into most appropriate, least restrictive forms of care. Screening systems—based on face-to-face evaluation, not paper review—need to be developed at least for Medicaid patients. Such screening might also be applied (as in Virginia) to self-pay nursing home admissions where Medicaid will be needed after only a few months.

Since a high proportion of nursing home patients come from hospitals, it's especially important that hospital discharge planning operations be strengthened and integrated with other agencies involved with long-term care. There should be incentives for them to carry out the most cumbersome tasks of arranging in-home services (and sometimes housing) rather than the simpler route of a nursing home placement. SSI rules should be changed so that rent or mortgage payments can be continued during a convalescent stay of several months in a nursing home, maintaining a home to return to. As chapter 4 showed, however, the major barriers to controlling the use of nursing homes are the limited supply of alternative care in many places and the control of access to scarce, publicly subsidized resources by private providers.

There is a good case to be made for expanding in-home care substantially. These proposals will draw strong political support. In 1981 the public supported an expansion of the present short-term and limited Medicaid home health benefit by a remarkable 87 to 8 percent.[5] Experience in some states and abroad has shown that patients just as impaired as those typically found in nursing homes can be cared for at home, usually at lower cost and to the much greater satisfaction of the patient. But home care is perhaps the most unevenly available and varied of all the major services for the aged. It is extensively available in some states, like New York, California, and Michigan. In many other states, little more than the Medicare benefit is available. This offers little or nothing for the chronically impaired, and new copayments have been officially proposed which would selectively deter the poorer elderly from using even the existing benefit.

During the mid-1980s, many states face severe budgetary pressures in maintaining home care, because of Title XX cutbacks and competing claims for state funds. States will seek to shift costs to Medicaid, to the degree that the federal government permits. Should Medicaid actually be federalized, the wide variety of home health and home care provisions among states would be a dilemma for federal administrators. They would be more likely to "level down" than to "level up."

Although expanded home care could prevent some nursing home costs, it is unrealistic to believe that it could be made available at zero or negative net cost. The reasons for supporting it are not primarily financial, but human. An expanded home care program would be a true "safety net," aiding the most helpless. It is important, however, that an appropriate funding and eligibility mechanism be chosen. Medicare, as a nationally uniform, federally financed program, would be a good vehicle, but only if a sliding scale of charges to the patient were instituted for this benefit. Meaningfully expanding the Medicare home health benefit would involve modifying the rule that "skilled nursing services" be concurrently required, the limitation to "part-time, intermittent" care, or both. A sliding scale would be a new and controversial element in Medicare, which has never included any kind of means-testing. But a benefit with no cost sharing would be prohibitively expensive: for example, if 10 percent of the elderly used an average of $3,000 annually in benefits, the cost could reach $15 billion a year. And a program imposing substantial cost sharing using the present Medicare copayment model—a non-income-related percentage of the cost of care—would be a benefit largely limited to the middle class.

Improving the availability of home care services under Medicaid is especially important for the poorest elderly, including those whose medical costs have impoverished them. Most states have not implemented the "personal care" provisions of Medicaid, adhering to more limited "home health" coverage. In 1980, New York State's program was accounting for about 80 percent of all home health and personal care expenditures under Medicaid nationally. The community care amendments of 1981 permit, in addition to the personal care services previously allowed, related services such as case management, transportation, and emergency call devices to be included in a state's Medicaid program for clients who would otherwise be eligible for institutional care. Their widespread implementation would be a step in the right direction.

But even where the needed in-home services are provided by Medicaid, its rigid financial eligibility provisions bar access to many elderly who need the care. In sixteen states as of 1981 the elderly and disabled living in the community could not become eligible for Medicaid, no matter how great their medical or long-term care needs, unless their income was so low that they were eligible for public assistance.[6] In such states, eligibility cannot be attained even by "spending down" on medical care the excess of income above the public assistance level. In almost all these states, persons with higher incomes can become eligible for Medicaid if they reside in a nursing home. Such sources of institutional bias should be eliminated from Medicaid. Even in the other states, Medicaid eligibility levels are so low (usually below 75 percent of the poverty line) that little is left to meet routine nonmedical needs.[7]

A bill to expand the Medicare home health benefit was introduced in Congress in 1981 by conservative Senator Orrin Hatch of Utah. The proposed legislation would provide for "homemaking" services and eliminate the skilled nursing requirement. It also includes, however, a copayment of 50 percent of the cost of the homemaking service. This major flaw would make the benefit inaccessible to those who need it most.

If the Medicare benefit is expanded, it will be important to move away from the medical model now reflected in Medicare home health services. As provided through Medicare-certified home health agencies, under relatively close nursing supervision, the current benefit often costs $10 per hour or more to provide. Under Title XX, states have usually been able to keep the cost considerably lower. Some have paid neighbors or friends to provide the care. Some provide funds to the client with which to hire an "independent provider"—a practice hotly debated in the field. In general, services provided through Title XX or the "personal care" provisions of Medicaid have been less expensive per hour of care than the more specialized and technical care classed as "home health services." We would be better off to define much of home care as a social rather than a medical service, and avoid overmedicalizing it. Pending a new financing mechanism for home care, Title XX isn't a bad one; and the consequences of Title XX cuts for long-term care and for the impaired and poor aged will be serious.

A Many-Splintered Thing

Another major policy and political decision for in-home services in coming years will be to define the role of for-profit agencies. It remains to be seen whether the home care industry will ultimately follow the proprietary-dominated pattern of the nursing home industry. Providing in-home care on the private market has already become big business; large national chains like Homemakers Upjohn, a subsidiary of Upjohn Pharmaceuticals, have emerged. These organizations have been able to exert considerable influence in state legislatures and Congress. They have succeeded in having the rules for participation of proprietary home health agencies in Medicare liberalized considerably, and will seek a major role in any expanded Medicare home health/homemaker benefit.

Finally, support of family caretaking efforts should become an important element in public policy. In 1981, the public supported a tax break to families that provide health care at home to the elderly, by 90 to 7 percent.[8] If structured as a tax credit rather than a tax deduction, and/or limited to families in financial need—either of which would distinguish it from most existing tax subsidies—such an approach might be one way to encourage these families. A better-targeted approach would be a system of respite programs which would provide the family with an occasional break from the responsibilities of caretaking; these now exist only on a scattered basis. SSI policies should be changed so that the elderly poor who live with family are not penalized by doing so, by having the assumed value of rent "deemed" as income and by having grants reduced to a lower "in the home of others" rate. These rules affect not only SSI income but also the Medicaid eligibility which SSI brings with it.

Acute Care

The cost of Medicare, primarily going to hospital and physician fees, has become a critical issue not only in old-age policy but in budget policy generally, as it approaches 7 percent or more of the entire United States budget. The projected cost of Medicare entitlements, as they existed in 1982, was $57 billion for fiscal year 1983 and $75 billion for 1985.[9] The majority of beneficiaries are middle class elderly (for the poorest, Medicare is irrelevant since they are eligible for the more inclusive Medicaid) and it escaped most of the cutting which other social programs experienced in 1981 and 1982. Chapter 6 showed how existing and officially proposed Medicare cost control measures work, by deterring utilization mostly by the poorest beneficiaries.

Realistically, some type of rationing is necessary; in fact, a major criticism of the existing measures is that they impose no marginal cost on elderly who have supplementary insurance. But flat deductibles and coinsurance are not a fair, or for that matter an effective, way to do this. If they are high, the poor cannot afford them; if they're low, they are an ineffective deterrent for the better off; in the middle, they're some of both. One approach would be to substitute income-related cost sharing, discussed above in the context of a new home care benefit, for some or all of the co-payments and deductibles for existing Medicare benefits.[10]

But exclusive reliance on patient cost sharing for cost control, even in this fairer form, ignores basic structural problems of the medical care system. Much of the most expensive medical care utilization, especially hospitalization, is at the initiative of the physician rather than the patient, and in coming years we will have many more doctors, ready and able to do more treating, hospitalizing, and operating. The general problems of medical care organization have particular impact on the elderly. Care is increasingly fragmented among specialists: fewer than a third of American physicians are in general or family practice or in general internal medicine, and 32 percent are in a surgical specialty.[11] Very few physicians are trained in geriatrics. House calls declined from 9 percent of visits in 1959 to .8 percent in 1975.[12] The elderly, more often than younger patients, have multiple and interacting problems, so the lack of coordination of care is a particular problem for them. The prototypical experience in visiting the homebound ill is the long row of pill bottles on the dresser, containing powerful medications often prescribed by different doctors, and about which the patient is often confused. Particularly for those who live alone, physicians are inclined to hospitalize the elderly patient when his or her condition becomes unstable or tests are needed. The high-speed pace of the typical doctor visit is ill suited to monitoring the elderly's multiple symptoms and to listening to and reassuring the older patient.

As the medical care system is presently organized, it is extremely difficult to control Medicare costs without actually denying badly needed care; in addition, care is often episodic, overspecialized, and lacking in a preventive focus. Rather than relying entirely on managing demand through cost sharing, a "supply side" solution is needed. Health Maintenance Organizations, responsible for providing comprehensive care on a prepaid basis, would be well suited both to equitable cost containment and to the better coordination of care. Plans like Kaiser on the West Coast have shown they can substantially reduce hospitalization when they have a financial incentive to do so, and they add an important preventive dimension to care. But only a negligible percentage of the elderly participate in HMOs; this is a result of Medicare's fee-for-service orientation, part of the compromise with the medical profession under which it was enacted. Existing HMOs cover only 4 or 5 percent of the total population, and are mostly based in employee groups; coverage is much smaller still among the elderly.

Medicare could make extensive use of HMOs, paying competing groups a flat per-capita amount per Medicare enrollee, set at or a little below the average total reimbursement for Medicare participants. The participant would agree to receive all reimbursed care, including hospitalization, through the HMO and would not have to pay deductibles and copayments. The HMO would have an incentive to minimize hospitalization and specialist visits, and maximize preventive care. In order to make this program work on a broad basis, given the limited number of existing HMOs, the Health Care Financing Administration would need, through start-up grants, loans, and the like, to foster the development of supply both through expansion of existing HMOs and through new "eldercare" organizations. Without such aid, a substantially expanded role for HMOs in Medicare is unlikely; but in the early 1980s even previously existing HMO grant and loan programs were being phased out.

Within an organized setting of this kind, use could be made of specially trained geriatric nurse practitioners, who could work in partnership with doctors, making house calls, providing routine medical care and check-ups, and monitoring patients more closely than a doctor would have time to. They would be able to listen to older patients, counsel them, and encourage good health habits. With additional training, public health nurses with experience in visiting nurse services could perform well in this role. Eldercare HMOs could also easily be integrated into comprehensive home care programs.

Limiting itself to financing care through fee-for-service, Medicare since its enactment has created much greater demand without changing the organization of supply. This helped to produce the enormous inflation of medical care rates of recent years. Medical cost inflation has hurt Medicare participants themselves: since Medicare doesn't cover all costs, they pay out of pocket more now than before. It certainly has hurt the non-elderly and the uncovered elderly, and frightened political leaders away from even thinking seriously about national health insurance. The HMO concept and other ways of revising the organization of medical care delivery deserve serious attention by Medicare, which is a major participant in the medical marketplace.[13] As the elderly population and especially the very old population soars, these issues take on added urgency. Medicare, to some extent, has become more indispensable precisely because of the problems it exacerbated, and there will be pressure to increase coverage. But it's not clear we can afford simply to have more of the same.

Income

Pension policies are central to the well-being of the elderly. Social Security and its problems have received the great bulk of public attention in recent years. The recent debate over Social Security has revolved around its ability to pay future benefits under currently legislated benefit and rate structures.

Some retrenchment in coming years seems inevitable, though politicians bob and weave in attempting to avoid taking the blame for the cutbacks. But unless the total retirement income system is dealt with comprehensively, restrictions in the public systems are likely to increase the trend toward two-class retirement. One group will have to rely on the public systems, work into old age, and retire into near-poverty; the other will receive multiple benefits, can retire early if they wish, and retire very comfortably. Already, there are two very differently situated groups. In 1980 elderly covered by pension plans other than Social Security had a median household income of $12,200 (and a mean of $15,800); those without pensions other than their Social Security received a median of $6,200.[14]

The proportion of retirees who can supplement their Social Security with other benefits will probably not grow nearly as much in the coming years as it has in the past two decades. Perhaps in part as an unintended consequence of ERISA, perhaps as a result of the slowdown in economic growth, the proportion of employees covered by private plans appears to have almost stopped growing. Under current policies, private plans will continue to aid the half of the aging that, by and large, is the best off. To the extent that members of this influential group are well provided for, their incentive to support the maintenance of Social Security benefits will be reduced.

The repeatedly proposed phased shift to a "standard" Social Security retirement age of 68, taking until the year 2000 or even longer to implement, does not meet with popular support thus far. In 1981 it was disapproved of by 59 to 35—much less popular than supplementing Social Security with general revenues, and little more popular than a means test for Social Security.[15] But this proposal might eventually prevail because it divides the opposition. Under the President's Commission proposal, anyone born after 1944 would have to work until age 68 to get full benefits. This divides the "baby-boom" generation from those now in and nearing retirement. Older people may be more concerned about these issues, since we tend to put off thinking about retirement until our fifties. As a manager in a pension consulting firm put it: "Congress now has to face up to the political reality and approve the change quickly, before the population ages further and political pressures against it increase."[16]

In spite of the lack of popular support so far, the proposal to push back retirement age in the future seems to reflect an emerging official consensus. Nearly all the various advisory groups and commissions that have studied the problem have plumped for it. There is logic in the idea, since in terms of remaining life span and even health 65 is just not as old as it used to be. But the advocates of most of these proposals, including the high-powered study groups, have failed to focus on the

178

necessary backstops to implement such a plan equitably. They haven't really dealt with the fact that a large proportion of the labor force now retires involuntarily, often well before 65—either because of ill health or because of unemployment.

Social Security, of course, provides a flat entitlement to a pension at a given age, regardless of any need-based consideration such as income (other than from employment) or ability to work. It would be fair to delay this entitlement if adequate need-based provision—through disability insurance and SSI, for example—were made available for those who really can't work that long. Disability insurance should help near-retirement workers who cannot realistically work at available jobs. Even if they do not meet the strict medical disability standards which are applied to younger workers, the physical ability to perform jobs that are actually available should be considered. Through stepped-up redeterminations starting in 1981, substantial numbers of beneficiaries were removed from the Social Security Disability rolls as well as from the disabled category of SSI, who had little or no practical chance of working. Without backstopping from disability programs, later Social Security retirement age could seriously hurt many who are unable to work. Similarly, SSI eligibility age should not be changed in tandem with Social Security retirement, remaining instead at 65.

Pension inequities will remain as long as the private system provides coverage—a chance, not an assurance, of a pension—to only half the work force, and as long as so many of those covered are unable to vest. The inequities will get worse if the public programs, both Social Security and the means-tested ones, are cut back without changes in the private systems. Enactment of ERISA established that tax-advantaged private pension systems are a creature of public policy, subject to regulation in the public interest. However, the compromise reforms of the Act failed to go far enough to affect the basic distributional characteristics of the system.

Only mandatory private pension coverage, along with immediate vesting,* would make the private pension system a truly equitable component of the retirement system. Of course, it would then look a great deal like Social Security, though with the very important difference that unlike Social Security it would be advance funded. Mandatory pension coverage, combined with required vesting and with existing funding requirements, would create a huge pool of new capital for the reindustrialization of America. Unlike the so-called "supply side" tax and budget cuts of the Reagan administration, such legislation would specifically channel resources to investment rather than consumption.

At any given time, about half the work force is in covered employment. A somewhat higher proportion work in covered employment at some time in their career, while a smaller proportion work for one covered employer long enough to vest. Mandated immediate vesting would end the forfeiture of private pension credits by workers who change jobs or whose involvement in the work force is intermittent. By itself, it would mean that 70 percent or so of the work force would ultimately get some private pension, though for some it would not be much of one. But immediate vesting by itself could lead to withdrawals from pension plans by employers, or reluctance to start new ones.

Mandated vesting would increase the pension costs of employers with plans, and would draw opposition from big business. Mandated coverage would hit smaller businesses with new costs, and would probably be sharply opposed in those quarters. Among the public, the idea of required coverage is popular; in one national survey, 80 percent of respondents felt employers should be required by law to provide a "reasonable" pension plan to employees.[17] However, neither reform

---

* The President's Commission supported these changes.

appears to have very good political prospects, at least in the short term.

In the absence of such change, private pensions remain a gamble and aid only an advantaged minority. Incremental reforms would help and would be well worth doing. An important one would be elimination of "social security integration" in tax-qualified plans. "Integration" concentrates benefits on high-paid retirees who have earned above the Social Security base. Incremental reduction in the required vesting period would be useful. But short of such sweeping changes, Social Security remains the keystone for assuring retirement income. It's an efficient mechanism, with administrative costs that are much less than popularly assumed, and less than those involved in marketing and administering a myriad of individual plans. (The advertising costs alone for IRAs are enormous.) None of the politically probable alternatives offer anything like Social Security's broad coverage, and those that offer individual choice are just not used by people who have to live from paycheck to paycheck.

The elimination of the Social Security minimum benefit for new retirees, in 1981, was a step in the wrong direction. Much better would have been to leave it in place but as a special benefit limited to retirees without other income. Rather than further cutting benefits—except for an indexing adjustment described below—a fairer way to cut Social Security costs and free up money which could be used to improve Supplemental Security Income would be to subject half the benefit to income tax. Presently, Social Security payments are untaxed, even for those with high retirement incomes. The extra tax deduction for the elderly is worth much more to high-income elderly. Altogether, relatively high income elderly are often in a very favorable tax situation, especially if they have a paid-for home.

The employee's share of Social Security contributions is taxed, but the employer's share is taxed no differently than income paid directly to the worker. The Social Security benefit can be seen as deriving from employee's contributions, employer's contributions, and attributed interest on contributions; only the first was initially taxed. By some estimates, as little as 17 percent of Social Security benefits derives from taxed income—though it is probably more reasonable to consider the equivalent of "interest" on the employee's half of contributions as deriving from a taxed source. It would be fair to consider taxing half of Social Security payments, for those with incomes above, say, $20,000 in 1982 dollars. This would be a more equitable way of achieving Social Security savings than most of the proposals which have been considered. With existing exemptions and standard deductions, people living only on Social Security would still pay little or no income tax, but those with substantial additional income, earned or unearned, would pay more.

So far, such proposals have made little legislative headway. But given the striking fact that a third of the public say they would like to see the entire Social Security program made into a means-tested one, and the widespread feeling that the program's costs are outstripping the resources to pay for it, there might ultimately be public support for recovering some of the cost through taxing benefits attributable to the untaxed employer's share for higher income elderly. This might especially be true if benefit reductions were, and were seen as, the alternative, and if the public had a better understanding of the real economics of aging.

Another reasonable approach, which apparently enjoys popular support despite official opposition, is the supplementation of the payroll tax with general revenues. Such partial general tax funding is typical in Europe. The Austrian system receives 35 percent supplementation, and general fund support is at 24 percent in West Germany, 23 percent in Belgium, and 15 percent in Switzerland.[18]

Over the next several decades, we can expect to see a growing conflict between generations over the cost of aid for the aged. This is already happening in states with a high concentration of old people, like Florida. Early in the next century, the United States will be "one big Florida"; in 2020 the national proportion of aging will be about the same as it is in that state now. Despite the pressures on income programs, kin will not be able to pick up the slack; if anything, the elderly will be even more independent of their families.*

Under financial pressures, Social Security is experiencing a crisis of confidence. For generations one of the most trusted governmental programs, it was expanded by almost every Congress until the late seventies. The realization that pay-as-you-go benefits can be adjusted downward as easily as upward has been a rude awakening. Insurance companies have taken to advertising their plans as the only guaranteed source of retirement income (gliding lightly over the unpredictable impact of inflation on privately invested programs). On examination, the current alternatives to Social Security fare poorly against standards of reliability or fairness, and their expansion could easily cost more than any savings in Social Security.

The "chain letter" effect that took place as Social Security expanded cannot continue indefinitely. The buck stops with the baby-boom generation, which will experience the reverse effect—higher contributions followed by lower benefits. To some extent, this is unavoidable; but the retirees of the next thirty years cannot expect a blank check from a generation whose own prospects in retirement are not good. Social Security reform should not be limited to those retiring in the next century. But drastic immediate changes would be unfair to people who planned on Social Security in good faith. An ad-

---

* Given that the economic contract between the generations seems to have been rewritten to some extent, it's also reasonable that we look at making it easier for older people to use their accumulated assets to live a little better on, rather than saving it all for their estates. The major asset of most older people is illiquid: equity in a house. Reverse mortgages can provide an annuity—monthly payments for life—in exchange for part or all of the equity. This deserves to be institutionalized, as it is in France where it is known as *le viager*.

justment that would be fair, but that would save billions and close much or all of the short-term gap between projected revenues and costs, would be to index grants by the lower of price increases and wage increases each year, instead of the present indexing strictly to prices. The incomes of Social Security pensioners would grow no faster than those of workers. Interestingly, unlike other proposals to cut Social Security costs this idea is supported by the public (by more than 2 to 1) and even by the elderly (by almost the same margin).[19] Also, without having to increase "standard" retirement age, we can adjust early retirement penalties and late retirement bonuses to encourage later retirement and reduce the number of years over which benefits are paid, as discussed in chapter 5.

In the Augustan age, Fulminius Minor wrote *non exstat prandium gratuitum*[20]—there ain't no such thing as a free lunch. This applies to pension plans. For a given level of expenditure into the system (in the short or longer run), one benefit provided is another foregone. As the demographic changes of the next few decades unfold, and the burden of pension systems becomes greater, the choices will have to be confronted more explicitly. The early retirement provisions of private- and public-employee retirement plans are expensive ones, since they very substantially increase the number of years over which benefits must be paid.

To a large extent, it has been the "actuarial bonus" resulting from the loss of accrued benefits by all the shorter term employees who fail to meet vesting requirements which has made high benefit levels possible. Other tradeoffs involve survivor benefits. Widows often get nothing at all, or a drastically reduced pension, when their retired husbands die; 72 percent of the poor elderly are women.[21]

As chapter 5 described, many private pension plans provide for retirement benefits at 55 and even earlier—often for highly paid managers and skilled workers who do not actually retire, but go on to second jobs. Tax sheltering should not be available to plans which provide such early retirement. This change would help to fund earlier vesting and would contribute to American productivity by putting needed skilled workers and managers back in the labor force, to the extent that they did not wish to finance retirement from taxed dollars.

Dealing comprehensively with pension policy involves addressing public employee pensions, individual plans, need-tested residual benefits, and disability programs, as well as Social Security and private pensions. Public employee plans often provide for retirement at unreasonably low ages—55 and even younger. The benefits of these plans, generous for those who qualify, are available only to those public employees who stay long enough to vest pension rights. Public employee systems, exempt from ERISA, usually have less favorable vesting requirements than are permitted for private plans—often fifteen to twenty-five years, with distributional consequences at least as significant as those in private systems. In addition, many of these plans are financially precarious, constituting a fiscal time bomb for the government units that sponsor them. Public employee pension systems should be brought over time under the same ERISA regulations which apply to private pensions.

The use of Individual Retirement Accounts and Keogh plans depends on a decision by the individual that he or she can afford to lock money away for decades, in exchange for tax benefits which increase with income. Their use depends on a certain level of financial sophistication, as well as on having discretionary income. As we've seen, under the law in effect prior to 1982, which limited IRAs to persons not covered by private pensions, and Keoghs to the self-employed, these plans were used overwhelmingly by upper-middle and high-income people. This was true for IRAs even though the population not covered by private plans is on average poorer than the covered group. In 1977 almost half the tax expenditures for IRAs and Keoghs went to the small number of individuals with incomes over $50,000.[22] Extending IRAs to people covered by a private plan, almost all of whom have Social Security too, will further advantage high-income people. IRAs are a wonderful tax shelter, and anyone in a high tax bracket is well advised to run right out and get one. But they won't assure adequate retirement for those who need help with this goal, and they drain revenue which could be used for those in greater need of assistance. The only justification of this expansion is that it might add to capital investment. But there are many ways of going about this; it's not necessary to use the IRA vehicle for that purpose.

To the worst-off aged, perhaps the most important government program is Supplemental Security Income (SSI). SSI is, in many respects, the stepchild of the Social Security Administration, accounting for only 1.5 percent of federal spending on the aged ($2.9 billion in fiscal year 1982). The basic federal payment represents a near-starvation income level; even after uneven state supplementation, income is usually well below the poverty line. Since supplementation is at state cost and the federal payment is so small, benefits have remained inadequate. Considering the probable financial condition of the states over the next few years, the squeeze will doubtless continue for SSI recipients, who by any measure are the "truly needy." The President's Fiscal Year 1983 budget proposal called for chipping away at these already miserly benefits—for example, by eliminating the income disregard which permits recipients $20 a month of other income.

Of all the various ways to invest dollars in benefits for the aged, perhaps the most important for those most in need would be to raise SSI benefit levels. The goal should be to raise grants to the poverty level. Federal minimums should be substantially increased, and the federal government should share in the cost of state supplementation on an open-ended basis. Finally, SSI should not penalize, as it does, the elderly who choose to live with peers or with family members.

Putting more income into the hands of the worst-off elderly would be a direct and efficient way of meeting many of their needs. In-kind programs and services certainly have a place, but income adequacy is basic: the poor know the relative value of goods and services to them better than officials and social workers.

The elderly on SSI are more likely to be old-old and health-impaired than the elderly generally. Despite Medicaid, they have many expenses related to their health—special diets, for example, and transportation to the doctor. A telephone for the frail elderly may be a safety necessity, not a luxury, yet many do not have one. In some cases, older people are forced into institutions through sheer financial inability to provide for their household expenses.[23] There is something paradoxical about providing sophisticated and very costly health benefits to the aged while providing for their other needs at a bare survival level. Increasing the floor defined by SSI grant levels would be an effective way of improving the welfare of the worst-off elderly. In an aging budget of $15,200 per aged couple, not counting tax expenditures, we can afford to provide a basic and adequate national minimum, above the poverty line, through SSI.

Private and individual pension plans are not the only "tax expenditures" related to aging. The extra tax deduction for the elderly is worth $2.5 billion annually: since its benefits are proportionate to one's tax bracket, it aids primarily the higher income aged. Since the bulk of the aged are no longer poor, there is less reason to provide benefits to older people simply because they're old. At least, the tax deduction should be provided in the form of a credit instead, and combined with the small existing special tax credit for the elderly. The exemption from capital gains taxation for sale of a principal residence after 55 is another substantial age-related tax benefit which is costly to the Treasury. And the exemption of Social Security benefits from income taxation, discussed above, is figured at a net cost of $12.6 billion annually (see appendix, table 20, for a list of tax expenditures for the elderly).

In income-maintenance policy for the aged, the principal choices, as we've seen, involve the relative roles of the private and public systems. Some argue, because of the difficulty in reforming the private system, that we should rely entirely on the public plans as the basis of national retirement income policy, and cut the tax advantages of the private ones. But there are some good reasons for trying to reform rather than giving up on private systems, not the least of which is that it's unlikely the existing tax benefits will ever be substantially reduced. The role of private pension funds in economic development is also important. One cause of our current economic troubles is the shortage of capital, exacerbated by low personal savings rates. Although the economic arguments are somewhat abstruse and there has been considerable debate over the point, it is plausible to believe that Social Security may have some negative effect on personal savings,[24] though not in proportion to the magnitude of the benefits. To make up for this, we should find ways to increase the degree to which pension plans, public and private, are advance-funded and thus create capital.

For Social Security, building up the trust fund, which is invested in treasury obligations, would reduce the borrowing requirements of the rest of the government and the resultant pushing up of interest rates and crowding out of private borrowers in the credit markets. Additional revenue sources for Social Security, such as a special energy excise tax, could produce this result. An energy tax would be a particularly attractive choice because it would foster conservation and reduce the need for oil imports and dependence on the cartelized oil exporters. Economist Martin Feldstein[25] has proposed moving Social Security to an advance-funded approach like some other public systems including the Canada and Quebec Pension Plans.

For private pensions, mandated coverage, immediate vesting, or both would have powerful effects on capital formation. Such steps would require that much higher sums be set aside each year to fund future obligations. Application to public-employee pensions of the vesting and funding requirements of the kind that now apply to private pensions, through a Public Employee Retirement Security Act (PERISA), would also create capital. It must be said, however, that the whole question of what determines savings and investment rates is not well understood by economists, and there is little consensus.

Since pension funds have become an important factor in our economy, it is appropriate that thought be given to their investment patterns. Pension funds have traditionally been invested in most cases in conservative securities. The institutional dominance of the securities markets steers capital away from riskier ventures. As Peter Drucker put it in one speech, investment is moving away from the entrepreneur who invests in the future to the pension trustee who invests in the past.[26] There is also a growing movement, especially by labor unions, to bring social as well as purely investment considerations into the management of pension money.

Social Participation and Mutual Help

I have argued that the potential of the extended family in the care and support of the aged has been overrated, and is declining as a result of external social changes including the expansion of the aging-welfare state. But the elderly have many needs for which government can do little directly. To whom can they turn when they have suffered losses of roles and relationships of earlier life through widowhood, retirement, the death of friends, and the moving away of family? Under appropriate circumstances, peer relationships can serve this function. The extent to which this is possible depends to a considerable degree on environmental and housing circumstances.

In old age, adaptive capacities decline; in many circumstances, the elderly who have lost social supports remain isolated. This does not have to happen, however, if the elderly find themselves in a situation that fosters the emergence of new social networks. Age-concentrated housing often leads to the emergence of mutual help networks which maintain morale and help the aged to remain safely in the community.[27] Such arrangements can also foster efficient provision of on-site services such as congregate meals and emergency call systems. Housing like this is common in England, where buildings are staffed by "wardens" on call. Serviced housing for the aged is unfortunately scarce in the United States; but age-dense housing even without services often can produce a remarkable level of solidarity and mutual aid among residents.

Criticism of age-concentrated housing as "segregation," often heard from planners, reflects a misunderstanding of the preferences of many of the aged themselves. The better-off aged can often choose to buy into a retirement community; the poorer aged seldom have this choice. A substantial investment in serviced housing, with rents held to a specified percentage of income, could improve the lives of many of the aged dramatically. Studies[28] have shown dramatic improvements in morale, health, social participation, and self-concept among elderly who moved into such housing.

For some of the aged, the workplace will be an important arena of participation in the future. Present work structures create an "all-or-nothing" choice for the older worker, particularly for managers. We assume that a career involves steady increases in responsibility, perhaps up to some plateau, and then total cessation of work at retirement. If the worker is no longer comfortable keeping up the pace, it is assumed the solution is to retire. Even if another assignment were available at a lower level, acceptance would usually mean a reduction in the pension ultimately available. In the interests of the older worker as well as other workers, including those of child-rearing age, we need to develop more flexible approaches to the world of work. Part-time work, or continued work at lower levels of responsibility, should be available, without reducing the ultimate pension entitlement. In the future we will need the skills of our older workers too much to push them out of the workplace when they wish to continue. We need to retain productive roles for the elderly. Employment programs providing for part-time opportunities in schools, day care centers, and in caring for other, infirm elders can improve the delivery of human services and enrich the lives of the elderly.

Aging Policy in a Changing World

The context of old-age policies has changed dramatically over the past two decades. Aid to the aged has moved from the periphery to the center of social welfare policy. In easier times aging policy could be all things to all people, cementing coalitions in which it seemed everyone could be a winner. This is less true today. In the coming conflicts over the costs of aging-welfare, pressures will be great on both sides. Reliance on benefit systems has become, in many ways, embedded in the social fabric. The constituency for programs for the aged will press for maintained and expanded services; others will begin to see programs for the aging as squeezing everything else in the budget.*

As these pressures are played out, what can we expect from public attitudes? Benefits to the aged have been remarkably popular. Public sentiment will probably support incremental adjustment rather than wholesale change. Continued public support for the expensive system of benefits seems to reflect a sort of contract among ourselves. We insure against some of

* Economist Rudolph Penner has described Social Security as an unfettered PacMan, insatiably gobbling up other social programs, in "Kowtowing to the Elderly," *The New York Times*, May 23, 1982, sec. F, p. 3.

the burdens of care we might otherwise feel responsible for as our parents age—and we expect that the benefits will also be there for us. In this sense the concept of "social insurance" can be seen as protection against obligation as well as personal need. This was epitomized in a political ad: "Merlino for Governor—so Joey won't end up having to take care of his old man."

It appears that both the elderly and their families find the reversal of childhood support roles stressful. Independence is especially valued by the elderly themselves. It is likely that support for the public role in meeting a broad range of the basic needs of the elderly will continue to be strong. But under budgetary pressures, the way we do this needs examination. If human services must be cut, it is poor policy to slash benefits for the needy aged and spare those aiding mostly the middle-class and higher-income elderly.

Old-age policy, like other social welfare issues, involves political competition among groups. In at least one important respect, however, the aged are a unique group: they are the one minority to which we all anticipate belonging. Broad public backing for aid to the elderly will continue, but the pressures of coming years pose difficult choices. The flow of resources to the older generation is there and will continue to be there. In managing it, however, we can and should do better.

Notes

Chapter 1

1. Zena Smith Blau, *Aging in a Changing Society* (2nd ed.; New York: New Viewpoints, 1981), p. 10.

2. Beth Soldo, *America's Elderly in the 1980s, Population Bulletin,* 35, No. 4 (Washington, D.C.: Population Reference Bureau, 1980).

3. Dominic Gagliardo, *American Social Insurance* (New York, 1955), cited in David Hackett Fischer, *Growing Old in America: The Bland-Lee Lectures Delivered at Clark University* (exp. ed.; Oxford: Oxford University Press, 1978), p. 142.

4. Marjorie Shearon, "Economic Status of the Aged," *Social Security Bulletin,* 1, No. 6, 1938.

5. Testimony of David Stockman, Director of the Office of Management and Budget, before the House Select Committee on Aging, April 6, 1981.

6. Joseph Califano, *Governing America* (New York: Simon and Schuster, 1981), p. 398.

7. Robert Clark, "The Influence of Low Fertility Rates and Retirement Policy on Dependency Costs," (paper prepared for the American Institute for Behavioral Sciences, 1976, available from author: North Carolina State University).

8. Alfred M. Skolnik and Sophie R. Dales, "Social Welfare Expenditures, Fiscal Year 1976," *Social Security Bulletin* 40, No. 1, 1977: 3; Edward Cowan, "Drive on Social Security Deficits Being Mounted by Congressmen," *The New York Times,* January 2, 1981, sec. A, p. 1. (Figures include disability benefits to some persons under 65.)

9. Health Care Financing Administration, *Data on the Medicaid Program: Eligibility, Services, Expenditures* (1979 ed.; Baltimore: Medicaid/Medicare Management Institute, 1979).

10. Robert Clark, "The Role of Private Pensions in Maintaining Living Standards in Retirement," National Planning Association Report No. 154 (Wash-

ington, D.C., 1977); James H. Schulz, *The Economics of Aging* (2nd ed.; Belmont, Calif.: Wadsworth Press, 1980), p. 150.

11. Merton Bernstein, testimony before Senate Subcommittee on Labor, June 21, 1972; U.S. Office of Management and Budget, *Budget of the United States Government, Fiscal Year 1982: Special Analyses* (Washington, D.C.: Government Printing Office, 1981).

12. Ibid.

13. U.S. Bureau of the Census, "Demographic Aspects of Aging and the Older Population in the United States," *Current Population Reports, Special Studies,* Series P-23, No. 59, 1976.

14. Lester Thurow, *The Zero-Sum Society: Distribution and the Possibilities for Economic Change* (New York: Basic Books, 1980).

15. Talcott Parsons and Renée Fox, "Illness, Therapy, and the Modern American Family," *Journal of Social Issues*, 13, 1952: 31–44.

16. John Henretta and Richard T. Campbell, "Status Attainment and Status Maintenance: A Study of Stratification in Old Age," *American Sociological Review*, 41, 1976: 981–992.

17. U.S. Bureau of the Census, "Money Income and Poverty Status of Families and Persons in the United States: 1980. Advance Data from the March 1981 Current Population Survey," *Current Population Reports*, Series P-60, No. 127, 1981.

18. Louis Harris and Associates, *The Myth and Reality of Aging in America* (Washington, D.C.: National Council on the Aging, 1975).

19. The followup to the 1974 survey was conducted in 1981 by Harris; results and survey documentation are in Louis Harris and Associates, *Aging in the Eighties: America in Transition* (New York: Harris and Associates, 1981), Project Director Elizabeth Montgomery, Senior Analyst Garry Nelson. The survey was conducted for the National Council on Aging, Washington, D.C. I thank the Harris organization and particularly Garry Nelson and Gordona L'Dera for the opportunity to review the planned survey instrument and make suggestions, and for expediting the access to the results.

20. U.S. Bureau of the Census, "Money Income in 1973 of Families and Persons in the United States," *Current Population Reports*, Series P-60, No. 93, 1974. Cited in Erdman Palmore, "The Facts on Aging Quiz: Part Two," *The Gerontologist*, 21, No. 4, 1981:431–437.

21. E. Fried, A. Rivlin, C. Schultze, and N. Teeters, *Setting National Priorities* (Washington, D.C.: The Brookings Institution, 1973), cited in Palmore, "The Facts on Aging Quiz: Part Two." The elderly, of course, are more than 11 percent of *adults*.

22. 1981 Harris-National Council on the Aging Survey, *Aging in the Eighties*.

23. Ibid.

24. Analysis by the author of 1974 Harris-National Council on the Aging survey data. See chapter 3, note 25.

25. Elaine Cumming and William E. Henry, *Growing Old: The Process of Disengagement* (New York: Basic Books, 1961).

26. John Demos, *A Little Commonwealth* (New York, Oxford University Press, 1970); Michael Gordon (ed.), *The American Family in Social-Historical Perspective* (New York: St. Martin's Press, 1978); Fischer, *Growing Old in America;* John Demos and Sarane Spence Boocock (eds.), "Turning Points: Historical and Sociological Essays on the Family," *American Journal of Sociology*, 84, Supplement,

Notes

1978; Alice Rossi, Jerome Kagan, and Tamara Hareven (eds.), *The Family* (New York: W. W. Norton, 1978); Howard Chudacoff and Tamara Hareven, "Family Transitions and Household Structure in the Later Years of Life," (undated paper, Clark University, Worcester, Mass.).

Chapter 2

1. Mary Jo Bane, *Here to Stay: American Families in the Twentieth Century* (New York: Basic Books, 1976), Appendix, Table A–1.

2. U.S. Bureau of the Census, *Census of Population: 1960, Women by Number of Children Ever Born*, Final Report PC(2)–3A, 1963; *Census of Population: 1970, Women by Number of Children Ever Born*, Report PC(2)–3A, 1973.

3. Beth Soldo, *America's Elderly in the 1980's, Population Bulletin*, 35, No. 4 (Washington, D.C.: Population Reference Bureau, 1980), Appendix, Table 2.

4. Health Care Financing Administration, *Long-Term Care: Background and Future Directions*, Discussion Paper, Office of Policy Analysis, HCFA 81–20047 (Washington, D.C.: Health Care Financing Administration, 1981).

5. Soldo, *America's Elderly*. In 1978, there were 14.3 million elderly women to 9.8 million men.

6. U.S. Bureau of the Census, "Demographic Aspects of Aging and the Older Population in the United States," *Current Population Reports, Special Studies*, Series P-23, No. 59, 1976.

7. U.S. Bureau of the Census, "Marital Status and Living Arrangements: March 1979," *Current Population Reports*, Series P-20, No. 349, 1980.

8. U.S. Bureau of the Census, "Demographic Aspects of Aging."

9. Ibid.

10. Estimated from data reported by Zena Smith Blau, *Aging in a Changing Society* (2nd ed.; New York: Franklin Watts, 1981), p. 12; and U.S. Bureau of the Census, "Demographic Aspects of Aging."

11. Soldo, *America's Elderly*.

12. W. Kip Viscusi, *Welfare of the Elderly: An Economic Analysis and Policy Prescription* (New York: John Wiley & Sons, 1979).

13. Robert N. Butler, *Why Survive? Being Old in America* (New York: Harper and Row, 1975), p. 24. Dr. Butler, head of the National Institute of Aging for a number of years, has made major contributions to the field, but in *Why Survive?*, like many advocates for the aged he did not give full recognition to the progress that has been made in the share of the national income going to the aged.

14. Robert B. Hudson, "Emerging Pressures on Public Policies for the Aging," *Society*, 15, 1978: 30–33.

15. U.S. Bureau of the Census, "Money Income and Poverty Status: 1980."

16. Lester Thurow, *The Zero-Sum Society: Distribution and the Possibilities for Economic Change* (New York: Basic Books, 1980) p. 159.

17. U.S. Bureau of the Census, "Characteristics of the Population Below the Poverty Level: 1975," *Current Population Reports*, Series P-60, No. 106, 1977.

18. U.S. Bureau of the Census, "Money Income and Poverty Status: 1980."

19. This was true both in 1972 and 1977: Thurow, *The Zero-Sum Society*, p. 53.

20. U.S. Bureau of the Census, "Money Income and Poverty Status: 1980."

21. U.S. Bureau of the Census, "Demographic Aspects of Aging."

22. Ibid.

23. Ibid.

24. Ibid.

25. The death rate from respiratory cancers among elderly white men was 423 per 100,000 in 1977. Women who are now elderly are much less likely to have smoked: their rate was 65 per 100,000. With the increase in cigarette smoking among women, we can expect this rate to rise in the future. U.S. Department of Health and Human Services, *Health: United States, 1980*, DHHS Publication (PHS) 81–1232 (Washington, D.C.: Government Printing Office, 1980).

26. Office of the Assistant Secretary for Health and Surgeon General: *Healthy People—The Surgeon General's Report on Health Promotion and Disease Prevention, 1979*, DHEW Publication (PHS) 79–55071A, Public Health Service (Washington, D.C.: Government Printing Office, 1979).

27. Ibid.

28. A study by Douglas Coate and Eugene Lewit of the National Bureau of Economic Research, described by Robert D. Hershey, "Washington Watch," *The New York Times*, January 18, 1982, sec. D, p. 1.

29. B. R. Luce and S. O. Schweitzer, "Smoking and Alcohol Abuse: A Comparison of Their Economic Consequences," *New England Journal of Medicine*, 298, 1978: 569–571, cited in U.S. Department of Health and Human Services, *Health: United States, 1980*, p. 26. Norman Ryder, "Notes on Stationary Populations," *Population Index*, 41, 1975: 3–28, cited in U.S. Bureau of the Census, "Demographic Aspects of Aging."

30. Ryder, "Notes on Stationary Populations." Even under this "adjustable definition," the percentage of the population in "old age" has been increasing. The proportion of the population in old age as defined this way increased from 35 in 1930 to 42 in 1960 to 44 in 1970.

Chapter 3

1. U.S. Bureau of the Census, "Marital Status and Living Arrangements: March 1980," *Current Population Reports*, Series P-20, No. 365, 1981.

2. U.S. Bureau of the Census, "Marital Status and Living Arrangements: March 1980."

3. Harold Sheppard and Sara Rix, *The Graying of Working America* (New York: Free Press, 1977), p. 33.

4. U.S. Bureau of the Census, *Census of Population: 1950, Characteristics of the Population*, vol. II, Part 1, U.S. Summary, 1953; *Census of Population: 1970, Persons by Family Characteristics*, Subject Reports, Final Report PC(2)-4B, 1973.

5. Albert Chevan and J. Henry Korson, "The Widowed Who Live Alone: An Examination of Social and Demographic Factors," *Social Forces*, 51, 1972: 45–52.

6. The estimate of parity effects is derived from a weighted linear regression of parity with proportion in families, with the parity groups as cases. The assumption of a linear relationship between number of children and living ar-

Notes

rangements accounts for more than 80 percent of the variation in living arrangements among the parity groups (using chi-squares).

7. The difference in fertility between the aged of 1960 and those of 1970 was .42 children per woman. Applied to our estimate that each child increases the odds of family living by 3 percent, this would account for about 1.2 percentage points of change, or about 9 percent of the actual change.

8. The analysis of coresidence attitudes is based on tabulations by the author of data from the General Social Surveys for 1973, 1975, 1976, and 1978, Principal Investigator James A. Davis, conducted by the National Opinion Research Center (NORC), Chicago. The data are distributed by the Roper Public Opinion Research Center, Yale University, New Haven, as a cumulative data tape, and were accessed through the on-line computer facilities of Project Impress at Dartmouth College. Frequency distributions for the years analyzed (and for 1980), along with documentation for the survey, are in James A. Davis, *General Social Surveys, 1972–1980, Cumulative Codebook*, distributed by NORC, July 1981. Approval for all those 18+ went up further in 1980.

9. "... the expectation that children should marry and produce progeny often conflicts with filial obligations ... just when parents become widowed and retired—that is, when they most need their children's solace and companionship—their offspring are deeply involved in their own marital, parental and occupational obligations ... When an individual has several role obligations, he must have priorities." Zena Smith Blau, *Aging in a Changing Society* (2nd ed.; New York: Franklin Watts, 1981), p. 49.

10. Anthropological literature suggests that institutionalized joking emerges around pressure points of role-strain in the social and family structures. See A. R. Radcliffe-Brown, "On Joking Relationships," *Africa* 13, 1940: 195–210. Radcliffe-Brown also suggests that vulgar jokes about the mother-in-law in our culture reflect structural tension in the parent-in-law relationship. He remarks on the number of societies in which distance is maintained from the parents-in-law in order to avoid conflict. See Radcliffe-Brown, "Introduction to the Analysis of Kinship Systems," in Norman W. Bell and Ezra F. Vogel (eds.), *Introduction to the Family* (rev. ed.; New York: Free Press, 1968).

11. Chevan and Korson, "The Widowed Who Live Alone."

12. The 1957 baseline data come from reanalysis of a survey conducted by NORC, and directed by Ethel Shanas, *Health of Older People* survey, NORC Study 383–A. NORC generously transcribed the data from the original multiply-punched cards onto tape and provided the data and the original study documentation from their files. Their help, and particularly that of David Cook, is gratefully acknowledged. This survey also forms the baseline for the analysis of change in financial-help attitudes.

The 1957 survey used a large national sample of 2567. An areally-restricted quota sample rather than a full probability sample was used, but the sample demographics conform well to census estimates. Other data from and documentation on the survey are in Ethel Shanas, *The Health of Older People: A Social Survey* (Cambridge; Harvard University Press, 1960).

In 1957, interviewers were instructed to minimize "it depends" responses by probing further for a "good idea" or "bad idea" preference. Since the Shanas survey included only respondents over 21, the GSS respondents 18 and over were excluded.

13. Samuel Stouffer and Paul Lazarsfeld, "Research Memorandum on the

197

Family in the Depression," Bulletin 29 (New York: Social Science Research Council, 1937).

14. The unavailability of nursing homes or other resources for care may have been one such pressure. Welfare policies sometimes pressured families into taking in an elderly relative, by demanding a financial contribution from the family if the older person were to live independently. Old Age Assistance was often refused to an older person whose family was considered able to take him or her in; see Alvin Schorr, *Explorations in Social Policy* (New York: Basic Books, 1968). Relatives'-responsibility provisions were included in Old Age Assistance rules in many states until the 1960s; Schorr found they were somewhat effective as a disincentive to going on welfare, less effective in terms of actual direct payments elicited. See also Robert Dinkel, "Parent-Child Conflict in Minnesota Families," *American Sociological Review*, 9, 1943: 370–379, for a discussion of the tensions in shared households formed under economic necessity.

15. The Harris polling organization made available to the author unpublished data from a number of survey items having to do with the aged. In 1965 and 1969 the following question was asked: "As an American, have you often, sometimes, or hardly ever felt bad because . . . of the way older people have been neglected?" In 1965, 38 percent of respondents answered "often" while 27 percent answered "hardly ever" or volunteered "never." In 1969, 52 percent answered "often" while only 12 percent answered "hardly ever" or "never," a substantial increase in the perception that older people were neglected (personal communication, Louis Harris and Associates). The strong response to the term "neglect" may be suggestive of an increasing perception of isolation as a major problem. As noted in chapter 1, the elderly are perceived as lonely. In 1981, 65 percent of those under 65 said that loneliness is a very serious problem for most people over 65, though only 13 percent of the elderly said it was a very serious problem for them personally. The elderly are perceived as poor also, but perhaps the public sees the government as capable of and therefore responsible for doing something about poverty, but not necessarily loneliness. See the discussion in the text of differential change in attitudes on coresidence and attitudes on financial help.

16. The interviews were conducted through random-number dialed telephone interviews in Boston, Rochester, and Houston. I am grateful to Professors Rainwater and Bane for making the interview schedules available.

17. Projects which have worked with family members who provide care for severely impaired elderly parents have reported that the demands and pressures can be severe. Considerable financial sacrifice, job interruption, restricted freedom, development of stress-related illness, and conflict among members of caretaking families is reported. See, for example, Dwight Frankfather, Michael J. Smith, and Francis G. Caro, *Family Care of the Elderly: Public Initiatives and Private Obligations* (Lexington, Mass.: Lexington Books, 1981). In unpublished findings, the Family Support Program of the Maryland Department of Aging added up the hours of care required and concluded that care of an impaired parent added up to more than the equivalent of a full-time job.

18. Marjorie Shearon, "Economic Status of the Aged," *Social Security Bulletin*, 1, No. 6, 1938. See also Shearon, "Economic Status of the Aged," *Social Security Bulletin*, 1, No. 7, 1938.

19. David Hackett Fischer, *Growing Old in America: The Bland-Lee Lectures Delivered at Clark University* (exp. ed.; Oxford: Oxford University Press, 1978).

Notes

20. Robert Dinkel, "Attitudes of Children Towards Supporting Aged Parents," *American Sociological Review*, 9, 1944: 370–379.

21. One major scholar, for example, asserted that there was a change in attitudes toward greater willingness to provide financial aid since Dinkel's time. He argued that the norm of financial independence between generations was being "modified by social changes which are conducive to mutual-aid patterns among generationally linked nuclear families" which contributed "increasingly to the maintenance of aged parents during the latter's retirement." He concluded that help from middle-aged parents to their children in the latter's young adulthood was increasing and served as a "way of buying kinship insurance during the period of old age," and that there was also an increasing flow of aid in the 1960s from middle-aged parents to grandparents. Marvin Sussman, "Relationships of Adult Children with Their Parents in the United States," in Ethel Shanas and Gordon Streib (eds.), *Social Structure and the Family: Generational Relations* (Englewood Cliffs, N.J.: Prentice-Hall, 1965).

22. Susan Grad and Karen Foster, "Income of the Population Aged 55 and Older, 1976," *Social Security Bulletin*, 42, 1979: 16–30.

23. Harris and Associates, *Aging in the Eighties: America in Transition* (New York: Louis Harris and Associates, 1981).

24. Analysis by the author of data from the 1974 Harris-National Council on Aging survey, "The Myth and Reality of Aging," distributed on tape through the Institute for Research in the Social Sciences, University of North Carolina, Chapel Hill. This study, conducted by Harris for the National Council on Aging, provides a large N of 2797 persons over 65, with a large oversampling of blacks, as well as 1457 persons between 18 and 64; it has been almost alone among data sources (other than the Census) in permitting detailed racial comparisons because of this. For survey documentation, see Duke University Center for the Study of Aging and Human Development, *Codebook for "The Myth and Reality of Aging," A Survey Conducted by Louis Harris and Associates for the National Council on Aging*, codebook and data tape prepared by Richard T. Campbell, Gloria Gardocki, John Henretta and Kristin Paulig, distributed by IRSS, University of North Carolina, Chapel Hill (undated). Further documentation, and other findings, are in the Harris survey report, *The Myth and Reality of Aging in America* (Washington, D.C.: National Council on Aging, 1975).

For further discussion of these financial help data, see Stephen Crystal, "Age-Group Relations, Social Change and Financial Help," (paper presented at annual meeting of the American Sociological Association, Toronto, 1981).

25. New York City Office for the Aging, "Selected Findings on the Black Elderly," paper prepared for New York State Seminar on the Black Aged, June 27–28, 1974.

26. For documentation of the Michigan Panel Study of Income Dynamics, see James N. Morgan, et al. (eds.), *Five Thousand American Families* (Ann Arbor: Institute for Social Research, University of Michigan, 1974).

27. Only 19 percent included adult children among the sources which "should be responsible" for the financial needs of older people when they are no longer working.

28. The model used was a multivariate analysis of percentage differences among groups by the "d-systems" method, as developed by James A. Davis from principles worked out by Leo Goodman and others. The method is documented in James A. Davis, "Analyzing Contingency Tables with Linear Flow

Graphs: D-Systems," in David Heise (ed.), *Sociological Methodology: 1976* (San Francisco: Jossey-Bass, 1975). Data on the specific findings from models produced for financial help and other aspects of extended family relations are described in Stephen Crystal, "Aiding the Aged: Social Structure, Public Policy, and Change" (Ph.D. dissertation, Harvard University, 1981).

In the model described for financial help, of a .25 difference in rates of financial help between whites and blacks, about a fifth, or .05, can be accounted for by income and marital status controls. However, it should be noted that a simple dichotomization of income as used here does not fully control for income. Within the "low" and "high" income classes, blacks are still worse off both in income and, especially, in assets. The difference by sex of .093 reduces to an insignificant direct effect of .037; the rest is accounted for largely by income and marital status differences between the sexes.

29. See also Crystal, "Age-Group Relations."

30. Sussman, "Relationships of Adult Children with Their Parents."

31. Matilda White Riley and Anne Foner, *Aging and Society, Volume I* (New York: Russell Sage Foundation, 1968).

32. Bernard Kutner, et al., *Five Hundred Over Sixty* (New York: Russell Sage Foundation, 1956); Alan Kerckhoff, "Family Patterns and Morale in Retirement," in Ida Simpson and John McKinney, *Social Aspects of Aging* (Durham, N.C.: Duke University Press, 1966), cited in Blau, *Aging in a Changing Society*. Blau summarizes the data suggesting that kin ties contribute relatively little to the morale of the aged. She sees the relationship between peers as inherently more equal and therefore more satisfying, while family ties suffer from a generation gap and from the difficulty in leaving behind earlier dependent/caretaker roles.

Another study reported that elderly with high expectations for help from children had lower morale than those expecting less—conceivably due to disappointment of these expectations: Wayne C. Seelbach and William J. Sauer, "Filial Responsibility Expectations and Morale Among Aged Parents," *The Gerontologist*, 17, 1977: 492–499. Like so much research in this area, however, this study was seriously flawed by problems endemic in much of the literature. These include the use of a catchall scale of extended family expectations incorporating very different elements; limited and unrepresentative sample; and applying control variables only one at a time, without assessing combined effects. In this study, the claimed relationship actually did not hold under various control conditions, including income and health, which largely vitiates the conclusion and interpretations.

33. Elmira study reported by Blau, *Aging in a Changing Society*.

34. Analysis by the author. Betas were .055 for recency of seeing children, –.044 for living with children, .141 for number of friends. Results from life-satisfaction scales should be interpreted cautiously, however. See chapter 6, note 33.

35. R. J. van Zonneveld, "The Netherlands," in Erdman Palmore (ed.), *International Handbook on Aging: Programs and Research*. Reviewed as pre-publication manuscript through the courtesy of the editor.

36. Ibid. Another report sets the proportion of older people living with "children or others" at less than 10 percent for 1970; Joep M. A. Munnichs, "Linkages of Old People with Their Families and Bureaucracy in a Welfare State, The Netherlands," in Ethel Shanas and Marvin B. Sussman (eds.), *Fam-*

Notes

ily, Bureaucracy, and the Elderly (Durham, N.C.: Duke University Press, 1977).

37. Ibid.

38. Ethel Shanas, Peter Townsend, Dorothy Wedderburn, Henning Friis, Paul Milhhoj, and J. Stehouwer, *Older People in Three Industrial Societies* (New York: Atherton Press, 1968).

39. Jerzy Piotrowski, "Old People, Bureaucracy and the Family in Poland," in Shanas and Sussman, *Family, Bureaucracy, and the Elderly.* The inefficient distribution of consumer goods in Eastern Europe may be one factor which makes shared homes advantageous; many Polish grandmothers spend hours every day waiting in food lines for the family.

40. Nada Smolik-Krkovic, "Aging, Bureaucracy and the Family," in Shanas and Sussman, *Family, Bureaucracy, and the Elderly.*

41. Palmore, *International Handbook.*

42. Erdman Palmore, *The Honorable Elders: A Cross-Cultural Analysis of Aging in Japan* (Durham, N.C.: Duke University Press, 1975).

43. Ibid.

44. John Creighton Campbell (Department of Political Science, University of Michigan), " 'Old People Problem': The Career of an Issue" (unpublished paper prepared for Columbia University Seminar on Modern Japan, February 18, 1980).

45. Susan Chira, "Retirement—Japanese Style," *The New York Times,* January 4, 1982, sec. B, p. 14. The estimate for percentage of elderly living with children in Tokyo comes from a Kyodo Press poll. Chira reports that there are now an estimated 70 retirement communities, all developed since 1976. She comments on a shift from traditional concepts which put a positive value on mutual dependence. Feelings among residents are reported as a combination of pride in independence and sadness at being unable to get along with children.

46. Erdman Palmore, *The Honorable Elders.* On the re-employment system, see Toshi Kii, "Recent Extension of Retirement Age in Japan," *The Gerontologist,* 19, 1979: 481–486.

47. The proportion of people 60 and over in the Japanese population is projected to increase from 8 percent in 1950 to 18 percent in 2000. This will recapitulate, at a faster rate, the population transformation which took place in the recent past for several European countries. Thus, the change from 8 percent to 18 percent which will take place over about a generation and a half in Japan took from 1800 to 1970 in France, and from 1910 to 1970 in West Germany and the U. K. Japanese planners expect increasing strains on their social institutions as a result of this rate of growth.

Japan's pension costs as a fraction of national income doubled between 1966 and 1975, though they have not yet reached the level of other industrialized countries. This was a higher rate of change than other industrialized countries, though the percentage increased there too during this period. For a number of the other countries, the most dramatic increases were for medical and long-term care for the aged rather than pensions, a phenomenon which has not yet hit Japan with full force because all but a very small proportion of the sick aged are still cared for at home. See National Institute for Research Advancement, *Japan Towards the 21st Century* (Tokyo, 1978).

48. The item was, "Which of the following do you feel should assume more responsibility than they have now for the elderly—the government, employ-

ers, religious and charitable organizations, the children of the elderly, or the elderly themselves?" (multiple response). Many respondents said they'd like to see both government and the children of the elderly assume more responsibility than they have now. However, a majority of the public (54 percent) specified government, while fewer (46 percent) specified children. Twenty-three percent thought the elderly themselves should assume more responsibility and 19 percent included employers. The notion that religious and charitable organizations should do more, in place of government, received little support; 14 percent mentioned this source. The elderly themselves chose government over children by 50 to 34 percent.

49. Schorr, *Explorations in Social Policy*.

50. The line between paying for an appropriate place to live and paying for medical care is not really a clear one. Under Medicaid, intermediate care facilities in particular provide basic living needs for the frail aged as much as health care.

51. U.S. Bureau of the Census, "1976 Survey of Institutionalized Persons," *Current Population Reports, Special Studies,* Series P-23, No. 69, 1978.

Chapter 4

1. Urban Institute, "Nursing Home Supplies and Demands, 1964–1974, Technical Proposal", RFP-187-75-HEW-OS (Washington, D.C.: Urban Institute, 1975).

2. Dava Sobel, "State Psychiatric Hospitals Forced to Change or Close," *The New York Times,* February 10, 1981, sec. C, p. 1; Stuart Taylor, "Curbing Civil Liberties of the Disturbed Is No Crime Cure: It May Be Worse Than the Disease," *The New York Times,* April 5, 1981, sec. E, p. 4.

3. A case from the Rainwater-Bane telephone survey data described in chapter 3, note 19.

4. National Center for Health Statistics, "The National Nursing Home Survey: 1977 Summary for the United States," *Vital and Health Statistics,* Series 13, No. 43, 1979.

5. Peter Fox and Steven Clauser, "Trends in Nursing Home Expenditures: Implications for Aging Policy," *Health Care Financing Review,* Fall, 1980: 65–70.

6. New York State Moreland Act Commission on Nursing Homes and Residential Facilities, *Regulating Nursing Home Care: The Paper Tigers* (New York: Moreland Act Commission, 1975), and other reports of the Commission; Bruce Vladeck, *Unloving Care: The Nursing Home Tragedy* (New York: Basic Books, 1980). Vladeck estimated that in the mid-seventies, nursing home fraud exceeded $100 million a year and may have run to several hundreds of millions a year. Embezzlement of patients' funds, he reported, has been widespread, and reimbursement fraud—in different forms in cost-related and flat rate states—was estimated at tens of millions per year. See Vladeck, table 5, p. 176, and discussion following.

A 25 percent cut in the federal appropriation for Medicaid nursing home inspections from 1980 to 1982, and a 50 percent cut for Medicare inspection, is expected to make monitoring of care quality harder; see Robert Pear, "Fund

Notes

Cuts Reduce Nursing Home Checkups," *The New York Times*, March 5, 1982, sec. A, p. 17.

Significant financial scandals, most visibly in California, have also taken place in connection with home health care providers.

7. "Nursing Home Briefs," *Modern Healthcare*, 11, No. 1, 1981: 106.

8. Health Care Financing Administration, *Data on the Medicaid Program: Eligibility, Services, Expenditures* (1979 ed.; Baltimore: Medicaid/Medicare Management Institute, 1979).

9. Vladeck, *Unloving Care.*

10. Ibid.

11. Health Care Financing Administration, *Long-Term Care: Background and Future Directions.* Discussion Paper, Office of Policy Analysis, HCFA 81-20047 (Washington, D.C., 1981) p. 15.

12. cf. Martin Rein and Lee Rainwater, *From Welfare State to Welfare Society* (Cambridge, Mass.: Joint Center for Urban Studies of MIT and Harvard, 1980).

13. National Center for Health Statistics, "National Nursing Home Survey: 1977 Summary."

14. U.S. Bureau of the Census, "1976 Survey of Institutionalized Persons," *Current Population Reports, Special Studies*, Series P-23, No. 69, 1978.

15. Health Care Financing Administration, *Long-Term Care*, p. 26.

16. U.S. Bureau of the Census, "1976 Survey of Institutionalized Persons."

17. Ibid.

18. Ibid., and U.S. Bureau of the Census, "Marital Status and Living Arrangements: March 1976." The long-term care survey applies to residents of long-term care institutions, excluding mental hospitals. About 96 percent of these are in nursing homes.

19. National Center for Health Statistics, "Differentials in Health Characteristics by Marital Status, United States, 1971-72," *Vital and Health Statistics*, Series 10, No. 104, 1976.

20. National Center for Health Statistics, "National Nursing Home Survey: 1977 Summary."

21. U.S. Bureau of the Census, "1976 Survey of Institutionalized Persons."

22. Ibid.

23. National Center for Health Statistics, "National Nursing Home Survey: 1977 Summary."

24. U.S. Bureau of the Census, "1976 Survey of Institutionalized Persons."

25. Ibid.

26. U.S. Senate, Special Committee on Aging, *The Multiple Hazards of Age and Race: The Situation of Aged Blacks in the United States* (Washington, D.C.: Government Printing Office, 1971).

27. Unpublished tables, National Center for Health Statistics, Long-Term Care Statistics Branch, Division of Health Utilization Statistics, "1973-74 National Nursing Home Survey," undated.

28. U.S. Bureau of the Census, "1976 Survey of Institutionalized Persons."

29. See, for example, Elmer P. Martin and Joanne Mitchell Martin, *The Black Extended Family* (Chicago: University of Chicago Press, 1978).

30. Daniel Patrick Moynihan, *The Negro Family: A Case for National Action* (Washington, D.C.: United States Department of Labor, Office of Policy, Planning and Research, 1965). Moynihan called attention to the effects of nu-

clear family instability on dependence on Aid to Families with Dependent Children. For the elderly, the effects may be different in some respects, at least in connection with the greater availability of help from coresident children (though divorce and separation also increase the proportion of black aged without a spouse's help).

31. U.S. Bureau of the Census, "Marital Status and Living Arrangements: March 1979," *Current Population Reports,* Series P–20, No. 349, 1980.

32. U.S. Bureau of the Census, *Census of Population: 1970, Persons in Institutions and Other Group Quarters,* Subject Reports, No. PC(2)–4E, 1973.

33. Based on a weighted linear regression, with the parity groups as cases. These data apply to elderly in group quarters, which, among the elderly, are mostly nursing homes and homes for the aged.

34. The change from 1960 to 1970 in number of children ever born for women over 65 was about .42; multiplied by the estimate of .5 effect in utilization rates for each child, the change might account for an increase of about .2 percent.

35. If 1960 rates of institutionalization within the 65–74 and 75+ groups had prevailed in 1970, there still would have been a 7 to 8 percent increase in the proportion of all persons over 65 who were in institutions, simply because more of the 65+ population was above 75.

36. The proportion of elderly living in the community who have impairments comparable to those of institutionalized elderly has been variously estimated, generally within the 5 to 15 percent range. See, for example, Elaine M. Brody, " 'Women in the Middle' and Family Help to Older People," *The Gerontologist,* 21, No. 5, 1981: 471–480. Estimates of the proportion of aged in the community who need home care range from 20 to 40 percent, depending obviously on definitions as well as on data sources. The high estimate is from Eric Pfeiffer, "Multidimensional Qualitative Assessment of Three Populations of Elderly" (unpublished paper presented at annual meeting of the Gerontological Society, 1973), but this estimate uses an extremely broad definition of need, and the data on which it is based, with different definitions, can produce a much lower estimate. Brody, reviewing the available studies, estimates one-third, but this again extends to the relatively slightly impaired.

37. General Accounting Office, "Home Health—The Need for a National Policy to Better Provide for the Elderly," Report No. HRD–78–19, December 30, 1977.

38. Health Care Financing Administration, *Long-Term Care,* p. 27.

39. Ethel Shanas, "The Family as a Social Support System in Old Age" (paper presented at meeting of the Gerontological Society, San Francisco, 1977).

40. National Center for Health Statistics, "Home Care for Persons 55 and Over, United States, July 1966–June 1968," *Vital and Health Statistics,* Series 10, No. 73, 1972.

41. Laurence G. Branch and Floyd J. Fowler, *The Health Care Needs of the Elderly and Disabled in Massachusetts* (Boston: Survey Research Center of the University of Massachusetts at Boston and the Joint Center for Urban Studies of MIT and Harvard, 1975).

42. General Accounting Office, "Home Health."

43. Ethel Shanas, et al, *Older People in Three Industrial Societies* (New York: Atherton Press, 1968) and Brody, "Women in the Middle." National Center

Notes

for Health Statistics 1966–68 data (NCHS, "Home Care") show that 87 percent of care was provided by relatives living in the household. Where care was provided by a paid provider, family members living outside the household paid for it only 6.5 percent of the time, again showing the relative rarity of "in-cash" rather than "in-kind" extended family help.

The 1977 Shanas paper, "The Family as a Social Support System in Old Age," showed that spouses were the source of care in the majority of cases; children, either in or outside the household, helped in about one-third of bedfast cases, and nonrelatives only rarely. Even in Massachusetts (Branch and Fowler, *The Health Care Needs of the Elderly and Disabled in Massachusetts*) and in New York, where publicly-funded home care programs are fairly extensive, the majority of personal care has been found to be provided through family members in the household. In New York, 77 percent of personal care services were reported to be provided by family members, usually female; Community Council of Greater New York, *Dependency in the Elderly of New York City: Policy and Service Implications of the U.S.-U.K. Geriatric Community Study* (New York: Community Council, 1978). James Callahan et al., in "Responsibility of Families for Their Severely Disabled Elders," *Health Care Financing Review*, 1, No. 3, 1980: 29–48, estimate that 70 percent of the disabled elderly live with others.

44. Brody, "Women in the Middle."

45. Dwight Frankfather, Michael J. Smith, and Francis G. Caro, *Family Care of the Elderly: Public Initiatives and Private Obligations* (Lexington, Mass.: Lexington Books, 1981); findings presented by the Family Support Demonstration Project of the Maryland Office on Aging, at a seminar on family support of the aged, Community Council of Greater New York, October, 1981. The Maryland project found that care of a severely impaired relative added up to more than nine hours of care per day. Frankfather et al reported that care obligations were usually concentrated on one relative, and that the emotional tone was typically one of a sense of obligation and fear of nursing home placement.

46. National Center for Health Statistics, "Home Care."

47. These responses are also from the Rainwater-Bane telephone interviews discussed in chapter 3, note 19.

48. Of children identified as next of kin, 46 percent reported strain on family relationships and/or conflict among family members before nursing-home placement; U.S. Bureau of the Census, "1976 Survey of Institutionalized Persons."

49. Sandra Newman, with James Morgan, Robert Marans, and Leon Pastalan, *Housing Adjustments of Older People* (Ann Arbor: Institute for Social Research, University of Michigan, 1976).

50. Joseph Heller, *Good as Gold* (New York: Pocket Books, 1979).

51. Newman et al., *Housing Adjustments of Older People*. Families who had placed parents in nursing homes were less than half as likely to be providing financial support as those caring for an impaired parent in their home. When a nursing home was used, public help was received four times as often.

52. General Accounting Office, "Entering a Nursing Home: Costly Implications for Medicaid and the Elderly," Report No. PAD–80–12, November 26, 1979.

53. Vladeck, *Unloving Care*, p.10.

54. Congressional Budget Office, *Long-term Care for the Elderly and Disabled* (Washington, D.C.: Government Printing Office, 1977).

205

Notes

55. Stanley Brody, Walter Poulshock, and Carla Masciocchi, "The Family Caring Unit: A Major Consideration in the Long-Term Support System" (paper presented at annual meeting of the Gerontological Society, 1977).

56. Martin Orr, "Development of Numerical Standards for Patient Placement in New York State Long-Term Care Facilities" (New York State Office of Health Systems Management, 1978). The discriminant analysis reported on in this paper, fraught with methodological problems, was used to assign weights to the various impairments. One result was the assignment of relative point scores which have no relationship to the prima facie relative severity of various conditions—two points for total blindness, for example, and eighty for inability to dress without help.

57. W. J. Foley and D. P. Schneider, "A Comparison of the Level of Care Predictions of Six Long-Term Care Patient Assessment Systems," *American Journal of Public Health*, 6, No. 11, 1980: 1152–1161. This study applied six systems to the same case profiles, finding little consistency in the results.

58. General Accounting Office, "Entering a Nursing Home."

59. Ibid.

60. Ibid.

.61. Ibid.

62. Thomas Coffman, in "Relocation and Survival of Institutionalized Aged: A Re-Examination of the Evidence," *The Gerontologist*, 21, 1981: 483–500, reviews the extant studies, quantifying in comparable format results from 26 relocated groups and reviewing other studies as well. While some studies show a negative mortality effect, others actually show a positive effect, and the averaged finding was no effect. The better planned moves had a slight positive impact, the poorly planned ones with dispersal of patient populations or poor staff morale a slight negative one, on average.

The question of transfer trauma reached the U.S. Supreme Court in 1980 in *O'Bannon v. Town Court Nursing Center* (100 S. Ct. 2467). The Court found that where state authorities revoke the Medicaid and Medicare participation of a nursing home, forcing patients to be moved, the patients do not have a right to a hearing on the certification question. In a concurring opinion, Justice Blackmun found that the alleged danger of transfer trauma had been unsubstantiated. See Coffman, "Relocation and Survival" and Elias S. Cohen, "Legal Issues in 'Transfer Trauma' and Their Impact," *The Gerontologist*, 21, 1981: 520–522.

63. William Scanlon, "A Theory of the Nursing Home Market," *Inquiry*, 17, No. 2, 1980: 25–41. This "decoupling" of supply and demand suggests that past projections of explosive growth in nursing-home beds, based on utilization trends and demographic change, are not likely to take place. In 1977, the Congressional Budget Office predicted a potential near-doubling between 1975 and 1985; Congressional Budget Office, *Long-Term Care*.

64. New York State Professional Standards Review Council, Press Release on Hospital Backup Study, New York City, May 20, 1980.

65. Health Care Financing Administration, "Long-Term Care," and Scanlon, "A Theory of the Nursing Home Market."

66. General Accounting Office, "Entering a Nursing Home."

67. Vladeck, "Unloving Care."

68. New York State Professional Standards Review Council, Press Release on Hospital Backup Study.

Notes

69. Health Care Financing Administration, *Long-Term Care*, p. 33.

70. United States Public Health Service, *Homemaker Services in the United States, 1958: A Nationwide Study*, PHS Publication No. 644 (Washington, D.C.: Government Printing Office, 1959).

71. Congressional Budget Office, *Long-Term Care*.

72. See Robert L. Kane and Rosalie A. Kane, *Long-Term Care in Six Countries: Implications for the United States*, U.S. Department of Health, Education and Welfare, Publication No. (NIH)76-1207 (Washington, D.C.: Fogarty Center for Advanced Studies in the Health Services, 1976); Alfred J. Kahn and Shiela B. Kamerman, *Not for the Poor Alone: European Social Services* (New York: Harper and Row, 1975); Alfred J. Kahn and Shiela B. Kamerman, *Social Services in International Perspective*, U.S. Department of Health, Education and Welfare, Social and Rehabilitation Service, Office of Planning, Research, and Evaluation, Report No. (SRS)-76-05704, 1976; Shanas et al, *Older People in Three Industrial Societies*.

73. See David J. Rothman, *The Discovery of the Asylum: Social Order and Disorder in the New Republic* (Boston: Little, Brown, 1971).

74. See Talcott Parsons and Renée Fox, "Illness, Therapy and the Modern American Family," *Journal of Social Issues*, 13, 1952: 31-44.

75. Home health care is provided by Medicare both under hospital insurance and supplementary medical insurance. Data for the former are extrapolated from figures for the first nine months of calendar 1980, in Health Care Financing Administration, "HCFA Program Statistics," Table I, *Health Care Financing Review*, 2, No. 3, 1981: 141. Data on the supplementary medical insurance portion are from "Quarterly Tables," Table Q-18, *Social Security Bulletin*, 44, No. 9, 1981: 77.

76. "No Place Like Home," television documentary, WNET-TV, New York, January 12, 1982.

77. Morton A. Lieberman, "Relationship of Mortality Rates to Entrance to a Home for the Aged," *Geriatrics*, 16, 1961: 515-519. See also Margaret Blenckner et al, "A Research and Demonstration Project of Protective Services," *Social Casework*, 52, 1971: 483-499. Blenckner et al reported that, as compared with a non-intervention control, a group of at-risk aged who received intensive social casework lived significantly less long on average because nursing-home placement was more likely to be arranged. There is certainly plenty of anecdotal evidence that nursing-home placement can have a devastating effect on morale and can cause withdrawal. As to a demonstrable mortality effect, the problems with the literature on nursing home transfer suggest great caution about relying on one or two studies.

78. William Pollak, *Expanding Health Benefits for the Elderly. Volume I: Long-Term Care* (Washington: Urban Institute, 1979).

79. Diane Carpenter Emling, *Adult Chore Services* (Lansing, Mich.: Michigan Department of Social Services, 1976).

80. Callahan et al, "Responsibility of Families for Their Severely Disabled Elders."

81. Office of the Director, Maryland Office on Aging, "Family Support Demonstration Project," undated project description.

82. Health Care Financing Administration, *Long-Term Care*, p. 10.

83. Ibid., p. 12.

84. Jacob S. Siegel, "Prospective Trends in the Size and Structure of the El-

derly Population, Impact of Mortality Trends, and Some Implications," U.S. Bureau of the Census, *Current Population Reports,* Special Studies, Series P–23, No. 78, 1979.

85. Margaret Dieck, "Residential and Community Provisions for the Frail Elderly in Germany: Currrent Issues and Their History," *The Gerontologist,* 20, No. 3, Part I, 1980: 260–272.

86. The best review of nursing home diversion projects is Jackson Knowlton, Steven Clauser, and James Fatula, "Nursing Home Pre-Admission Screening: A Review of State Programs," *Health Care Financing Review,* 3, No. 3, 1982: 75–87. Twenty-eight states and the District of Columbia were reported as having pre-assessment screening programs in place for Medicaid patients. Virginia's program is of particular interest because it extended to non-hospitalized individuals who planned to enter on a self-pay basis but were expected to become eligible for Medicaid within 90 days. The State reported that approximately 20 percent of cases screened were not approved for nursing home placement and that they are considering two significant changes in the screening program. The first would extend its scope to hospitalized patients, and the second would require any individual with less than 13 months of funds available for nursing home care to be screened before admission.

Chapter 5

1. Employee Benefit Research Institute, *Demographics and Inflation: Cause for Concern Over Retirement Income Policy* (Washington, D.C.: Employee Benefit Research Institute, 1980).

2. U.S. Office of Management and Budget, *Budget of the United States Government, Fiscal Year 1982: Special Analyses* (Washington, D.C.: Government Printing Office, 1981).

3. President's Commission on Pension Policy, *Coming of Age: Toward a National Retirement Income Policy, Final Report* (Washington, D.C.: Government Printing Office, 1981). Actually, the Commission estimated the percentage of aged receiving at least some "retirement income" at more than 97 percent!

4. *Social Security Bulletin,* November 1977, p. 27. Cited in President's Commission on Pension Policy, *Final Report,* p.12.

5. Findings both from a survey done for the President's Commission on Pension Policy and from a joint survey by the Department of Labor and the Social Security Administration, reported in President's Commission on Pension Policy, *Interim Report* (Washington, D.C.: Government Printing Office, May 1980).

6. Ibid.

7. The budget figures come from U.S. Office of Management and Budget, *Budget of the United States: Fiscal Year 1982,* and from a letter to the author from Special Studies Division, Office of Management and Budget, February 12, 1981. The self-declaration system for veterans' pensions is discussed in David E. Rosenbaum, "Veterans Programs Escaping Budget Trims Despite Criticism of Some Benefits," *The New York Times,* February 22, 1981, sec. A, p. 1.

8. U.S. Office of Management and Budget, *Budget of the United States, Fiscal Year 1982, Special Analyses.*

Notes

9. U.S. Senate, Committee on the Budget, *Tax Expenditures: Relationships to Spending Programs and Background Materials on Individual Provisions* (Washington, D.C.: Government Printing Office, 1978).

10. U.S. Office of Management and Budget, *Budget of the United States, Fiscal Year 1983, Special Analysis G, Tax Expenditures* (Washington, D.C.: Government Printing Office, 1982), Table G-1, p. 28.

11. President's Commission on Pension Policy, *Final Report*, pp. 14–15. Because of the skewed distribution of income among the aged (an indication of the high level of inequality), the percentage of aggregate income accounted for by Social Security is about 40, yet Social Security accounts for more than 50 percent of the income of a person with income at the median of the distribution. At the $4,000 income level, Social Security accounts for 75 percent of income. The 40 percent figure comes from James Schulz, in testimony summarized in "The People Speak" section of the *Final Report*, p. 82.

12. President's Commission on Pension Policy, *Interim Report*, May 1980. It is unclear whether the minimum-wage calculations were affected by the Social Security minimum benefit which was revoked for new retirees in 1981. If so, the degree of redistribution may now be less than these figures indicate.

13. James Jorgensen, *The Graying of America: Retirement and Why You Can't Afford It* (New York: McGraw-Hill, 1980).

14. Ibid.

15. President's Commission on Pension Policy, *Final Report*, p. 23.

16. From a 1982 staff report of the Senate Special Committee on Aging, described by Warren Weaver, "Europeans' Pensions Rely on General Funds," *The New York Times*, January 17, 1982, sec. A, p. 21.

17. Warren Weaver, "Poll Shows Americans Losing Faith in Future of Social Security System," *The New York Times*, July 17, 1981, sec. A, p. 12.

18. Social Security Administration, "Erroneous Public Perception of SSA Administrative Expenses," *Social Security Bulletin*, 44, No. 9, 1981: 1.

19. Ibid., from Annual Reports of the Social Security Trust Funds.

20. U.S. Securities and Exchange Commission, Directorate of Economic and Policy Analysis, "Assets of Private and Public Pension Funds," press release, August 12, 1980.

21. Merton Bernstein, *The Future of Private Pensions* (New York: Macmillan, 1964).

22. Ibid., and James H. Schulz, *The Economics of Aging* (2nd ed.; Belmont, Calif.: Wadsworth Publishing Company, 1980).

23. Robert Clark, *The Role of Private Pensions in Maintaining Living Standards in Retirement*, National Planning Association Report No. 154 (Washington, D.C., 1977).

24. Ibid.

25. Jorgensen, *The Graying of America*, p. 124.

26. Karen W. Arenson, "The 25 Percent of 'Expenditures' Washington Never Sees," *The New York Times*, February 7, 1982, sec. E, p. 4.

27. Stephen Crystal, "Distributional Issues in the Private Pension System," (unpublished manuscript, Harvard University), quoted in David Hapgood, *The Screwing of the Average Man* (New York: Bantam Books, 1975).

28. Bernstein, *The Future of Private Pensions.*

29. President's Commission on Pension Policy, *Final Report*, p. 13, based on its 1979 household survey. The findings on differences by sex are matched

closely by data reported by the Commission from Department of Labor and other sources; see, for example, Walter W. Kolodrubetz and Donald M. Landay, "Coverage and Vesting of Full-Time Employees Under Private Retirement Plans," *Social Security Bulletin,* November, 1973: 20–36.

30. Gayle B. Thompson, "Black-White Differences in Private Pensions: Findings From the Retirement History Study," *Social Security Bulletin,* 42, No. 2, 1979: 15–36.

31. President's Commission on Pension Policy, *Interim Report,* May, 1980.

32. U.S. Department of Labor, Bureau of Labor Statistics, "Average Job Tenure Declines," press release, April 23, 1979. Kolodrubetz and Landay, "Coverage and Vesting of Full-Time Employees," report similar differences in job tenure by sex (longer for both sexes) in 1968–69.

33. Walter Kolodrubetz, "Private Retirement Benefits and Relationship to Earnings: Survey of New Beneficiaries," *Social Security Bulletin,* May, 1973: 16.

34. Thompson, "Black-White Differences in Private Pensions."

35. U.S. Senate, Committee on the Budget, *Tax Expenditures.* Findings from Congressional Budget Office.

36. Clark, *Role of Private Pensions.*

37. Philip Davis and David C. Lewis, *So You Think You Have a Pension Plan* (New York: Secretarial Publishing Company, 1969).

38. Alan Walker, "The Social Creation of Poverty and Dependency in Old Age," *Journal of Social Policy,* 9, No. 1, 1980: 49–75.

39. John Myles, "The Aged, the State, and the Structure of Inequality," in John Harp and John Hofley (eds.), *Structured Inequality in Canada* (Toronto: Prentice-Hall, 1980).

40. Kolodrubetz, "Private Retirement Benefits."

41. Leif Haanes-Olsen, "Earnings-Replacement Rate of Old-Age Benefits, 1965–75, Selected Countries," *Social Security Bulletin,* 46, No. 1, 1978: 3–4.

42. Peter F. Drucker, *The Unseen Revolution: How Pension Fund Socialism Came to America* (New York: Harper & Row, 1976), expanded version of Drucker, "Pension Fund 'Socialism,' " *The Public Interest,* 42, 1976: 3–46.

43. Ibid.

44. Urban Institute, "The Future of State and Local Pensions," summarized in Thomas J. Cavanaugh and Richard J. Murphy, "Urban Institute's Report on State and Local Pensions," *Pension World,* 17, No. 10, 1981: 39–42.

45. Jorgensen, *The Graying of America,* p. 145.

46. Robert Lindsey, "Soaring Pension Costs Termed Key Factor in Proposed Layoffs on Coast," *The New York Times,* April 26, 1981, sec. A, p. 30.

47. President's Commission on Pension Policy, *Final Report,* p. 18.

48. Ibid., p. 19.

49. City of New York, *Official Statement for General Obligation Bonds,* November 25, 1981.

50. U.S. Office of Management and Budget, *Budget of the United States, Fiscal Year 1983, Special Analysis G.*

51. U.S. Senate, Committee on the Budget, *Tax Expenditures.*

52. U.S. Treasury Department data reported in *BNA Pension Reporter,* February 20, 1978, R–9, cited in James Schulz, *The Economics of Aging.*

53. President's Commission on Pension Policy, *Interim Report,* November, 1980.

54. Schulz, *The Economics of Aging,* p. 150.

Notes

55. "Pension Power," *New York Daily News*, September 11, 1981; see also estimates in Drucker, *The Unseen Revolution*.

56. Drucker, *The Unseen Revolution*.

57. The President's Commission on Pension Policy, among others, called attention to this as a possible problem, but it is extraordinary how little research there has been on the effects of pension investment patterns.

58. Myles, "The Aged, the State and the Structure of Inequality."

59. Ibid.

60. Geoffrey Calvert, "Pensions, and Survival: The Coming Crisis of Money and Retirement," *Financial Post*, 71, 1977: 35, cited in Myles, "The Aged, the State, and the Structure of Inequality."

61. Ad campaign of Aetna Life Insurance.

62. U.S. Bureau of the Census, "Demographic Aspects of Aging and the Older Population in the United States," *Current Population Reports, Special Studies*, Series P–23, No. 59, 1976.

63. President's Commission on Pension Policy, *Final Report*, p. 36.

64. U.S. Bureau of the Census, "Demographic Aspects of Aging."

65. President's Commission on Pension Policy, *Final Report*, p. 36.

66. Ibid., p. 23.

67. "The Hidden Cost of Federal Pensions," *Business Week*, April 27, 1974. Similarly estimated by the President's Commission on Pension Policy in its *Final Report*.

68. James Gollin, *The Star-Spangled Retirement Dream* (New York: Scribner, 1981), p. 163.

69. Ibid., and President's Commission on Pension Policy, *Final Report*.

70. W. Kip Viscusi, *Welfare of the Elderly: An Economic Analysis and Policy Prescription* (New York: John Wiley & Sons, 1979).

71. Herbert Gold, "Job Is the New Neighborhood," *Apartment Life*, March, 1980: 30–34.

72. 1981 Harris-National Council on the Aging survey.

73. Viscusi, "Welfare of the Elderly."

74. Richard F. Wertheimer and Shiela R. Zedlewski, *The Aging of America:·A Portrait of the Elderly in 1990*, Working Paper 1224–01 (Washington, D.C.: Urban Institute, 1978).

75. Ibid. The microsimulation economic model they used produced an estimate of four million more elderly in the labor force as a result of these measures and "pro-employment economic policies," but, unfortunately, they do not tell us what the projected effect of the Social Security changes alone would be.

76. Bankers Trust Company of New York, *1975 Study of Corporate Pension Plans* (New York: Bankers Trust Co., 1975).

77. Data from Bureau of Labor Statistics study of reports filed with federal regulatory authorities, reported in Harry E. Davis, "Multiemployer Pension Plan Provisions in 1973," *Monthly Labor Review*, October, 1974, and cited in Alfred M. Skolnik, "Private Pension Plans, 1950–74," *Social Security Bulletin*, June, 1976: 3–17.

78. Skolnik, "Private Pension Plans, 1950–74," based on Bureau of Labor Statistics surveys.

79. Results of a Conference Board study of 641 manufacturers in 1970, reported in Mitchell Meyer and Harlan Fox, *Early Retirement Programs* (New York:

The Conference Board, 1971), and cited in Clark, *Role of Private Pensions*.

Another way private pension plans encourage workers to retire earlier than they otherwise would is by "freezing" pensions at 65, refusing to continue giving credit for years of work after that age. Approximately half of plans freeze benefits at 65 in this way, according to the accounting firm Peat, Marwick, Mitchell and Co.; see Jill Bettner, "Will Your Pension Work Past 65 If You Do?" *The Wall Street Journal*, April 5, 1982, p. 44. Far fewer, probably less than one percent, make an actuarial adjustment for late retirees to adjust for the fact that they will receive the pension, on average, for fewer years. Thus nearly all private pension beneficiaries, even those whose benefits are not frozen, do not receive full credit for work past 65. ERISA does not prohibit such freezing of benefits at 65.

80. Again, the "two-class system" is not unique to the United States or even to capitalism. After the liberalization instigated by the Solidarity movement, Zygmunt Nagorski interpreted the 1981 imposition of martial law in Poland as a counterrevolution of the privileged "new class" whose "most blatantly unfair perquisite" has been its retirement benefits. Notably, this privileged group—senior party members, high-level industrial managers, policemen, the security forces, and the upper echelons of the army—has been eligible for considerably earlier retirement than ordinary workers. Nagorski, "Counterrevolution," *The New York Times*, December 30, 1981, sec. A, p. 15.

81. 1981 Harris-National Council on the Aging Survey.

82. Ibid.

83. Ibid.

Chapter 6

1. *1980 Annual Report of the Board of Trustees of the Social Security Trust Funds*, cited in President's Commission on Pension Policy, *Coming of Age: Toward a National Retirement Income Policy: Final Report* (Washington, D.C.: Government Printing Office, 1981), p. 23.

2. Social Security Administration, "Current Operating Statistics," Table M–13, *Social Security Bulletin*, 44, No. 9, 1981: 31.

3. Martha Derthick, in her definitive study of these events, *Policymaking for Social Security* (Washington: Brookings Institution, 1979), says, "Political leaders did not perceive the implications of the . . . formula, and the program specialists, who did understand them, took no pains to point them out."

4. James Gollin, *The Star-Spangled Retirement Dream* (New York: Charles Scribner's Sons, 1981), p. 125.

5. Testimony of David Stockman, Director of the Office of Management and Budget, before the House Select Committee on Aging, April 6, 1981.

6. David L. Klemmack and Lucinda L. Roff, in "Predicting General and Comparative Support for Government's Providing Benefits to Older Persons," *The Gerontologist*, 21, No. 6, 1981: 592–599, asked a sample of Alabama residents to allocate hypothetical "budget points" among various kinds of services. Their allocations gave more to disabled persons, the non-elderly poor,

Notes

and education, and less to benefits to older people like Medicare and Social Security, than does the actual budget.

7. Stockman, testimony before the House Select Committee on Aging.

8. Robert Clark, "The Influence of Low Fertility Rates and Retirement Policy on Dependency Costs," (paper prepared for the American Institutes for Behavioral Sciences, available from author: North Carolina State University).

9. 1981 Harris-National Council on the Aging Survey, reported in Louis Harris and Associates, *Aging in the Eighties: America in Transition* (New York, 1981).

10. The percentages of those near retirement—55 to 64—who had taken five or more of the retirement preparation steps were 33 for those with household income under $10,000, 76 for those over $35,000; 31 for the least educated, 69 for the most; 56 for whites, 19 for blacks, 22 for Hispanics.

11. Lester Thurow, *The Zero-Sum Society: Distribution and the Possibilities for Economic Change* (New York: Basic Books, 1980).

12. Susan Grad and Karen Foster, "Income of the Population Aged 55 and Older," *Social Security Bulletin*, 42, No. 7, 1976: 16–31; President's Commission on Pension Policy, *Interim Report* (Washington, D.C.: Government Printing Office, November 1980).

13. Ibid.

14. See, for example, Henry J. Pratt, *The Gray Lobby* (Chicago: University of Chicago Press, 1976).

15. 1981 Harris-National Council on the Aging survey.

16. Ibid.

17. Karen Davis, "Equal Treatment and Unequal Benefits: The Medicare Program," *Milbank Memorial Fund Quarterly (Health and Society)*, 53, 1975: 449–488.

18. Ibid.

19. A later study followed up on Davis' report, which was based on 1968 and 1969 data, for racial differences but not, unfortunately, for differences in utilization by income. It found that the gap had narrowed, though not disappeared, by 1976. Total reimbursement per enrollee in 1976 was 10 percent greater for whites than nonwhites, despite the poorer health status of nonwhite elderly. These data, though showing improvement, also showed the differential specific effect of deductibles on nonwhite utilization. Nonwhites were less likely than whites to surmount the deductible and thus receive any reimbursement, by 13 percent. Once they had done so they received about 3 percent more reimbursement on average.

This trend to improvement in equity may well be reversed as a result of the increases in cost sharing in 1981, and the further increases which are likely. It is interesting to note that the rate of utilization of the nursing-home benefit was 72 percent greater in 1976 for whites, but utilization of the home-care benefit was 14 percent greater for nonwhites. This, along with the analysis presented in chapter 4, suggests that improvements in home-care benefits can redress, to some extent, the problems of equity which result from underutilization by nonwhites of institutional long-term care. Martin Ruther and Allen Dobson, "Equal Treatment and Unequal Benefits: A Re-examination of the Use of Medicare Services by Race, 1967–1976," *Health Care Financing Review*, 2, No. 3, 1981: 55–83.

20. The 1981 Harris survey found that 21 percent of the lowest income elderly had not seen a doctor when there was something about their health that made them feel they should have. This was true for only 8 percent of the highest income elderly. Of these, 50 percent of low income elderly, and 17 percent of the elderly in the highest bracket reported, said they did not do so because it was too expensive.

21. Ruther and Dobson, "Equal Treatment and Unequal Benefits."

22. Quoted in Aaron Wildavsky, "Doing Better and Feeling Worse: The Political Pathology of Health Policy," *Daedalus*, Winter, 1977: 105–123.

23. Vivian Gornick, "Things Can Only Get Worse," in Ronald Gross, Beatrice Gross and Sylvia Seidman, *The New Old: Struggling for Decent Aging* (Garden City, N.Y.: Anchor Books, 1978), p. 33.

24. See Martha Derthick, *Uncontrollable Spending for Social Services Grants* (Washington, D.C.: Brookings Institution, 1975).

25. Robert B. Hudson, "Emerging Pressures on Public Policies for the Aging," *Society*, 15, 1978: 30–33.

26. Carroll Estes, *The Aging Enterprise: A Critical Examination of Social Policies and Services for the Aged* (San Francisco: Jossey-Bass, 1979).

27. Alan Walker, "The Social Creation of Poverty and Dependency in Old Age," *Journal of Social Policy*, 9, No. 1, 1980: 49–75.

28. Thurow, *The Zero-Sum Society*, p. 52. See also John Henretta and Richard T. Campbell, "Status Attainment and Status Maintenance: A Study of Stratification in Old Age," *American Sociological Review*, 41, 1976: 981–992; and U.S. Bureau of the Census, "Trends in Money Income of Persons and Families, 1929–1964," Technical Paper No. 19, 1967. Schulz, *The Economics of Aging*, provides general data and discussion on the income distribution among the aged.

29. Henretta and Campbell, "Status Attainment and Status Maintenance."

30. U.S. Bureau of the Census, "Trends in Money Income of Persons and Families, 1929–1964."

31. The study used the Havighurst Life Satisfaction Index Z. See Linda K. George and Lucille B. Bearon, *Quality of Life in Older Persons: Meaning and Measurement* (New York: Human Sciences Press, 1980), for documentation and analysis of this scale and for a review generally of the difficult conceptual and methodological problems surrounding life-satisfaction and related indices. 1974 mean scores in the Harris survey were 22.7 in the lowest income bracket, and 29.4 for the highest. In 1981 (brackets roughly adjusted for inflation) those in the lowest bracket averaged only 19.9 on the same scale, and those in the highest bracket 28.4. Whites averaged 25.1 to 22.3 for blacks: the difference disappeared when income was controlled. College graduates scored 28.4 versus 22.2 for those who did not graduate from high school. Those in the labor force scored 28.0 versus 24.8 for those who had retired (who were, of course, older on average).

32. This distinction was made by Reagan Budget Director David Stockman in a famous *Atlantic Monthly* article. Stockman acknowledged to his interviewer that the Reagan administration, in its first year, had chosen strong clients with weak claims over the converse in budget and taxation policy generally. William Greider, "The Education of David Stockman," *Atlantic Monthly*, December, 1981.

Notes

33. Arnold Relman, "The New Medical-Industrial Complex," *New England Journal of Medicine*, October 23, 1980.

Chapter 7

1. For example, consider the following from a 1968 New York State Division of Mental Health directive, setting new and much more restrictive admission standards: "We are convinced that the long-term result of such a program will be the development of services for those we refuse. . . ." Presumably this was someone else's responsibility, and could be done *after* the institutions were phased down. Earlier the directive states that accepting patients considered unsuitable "removes from the community the necessity for developing adequate services to solve these problems." From Division of Mental Health Memorandum 68–27, which was followed by massive diversion and dumping of patients; cited in New York State Moreland Act Commission, "Assessment and Placement: Anything Goes," Commission Report 6, 1976. The Moreland Commission's discussion of mental hospital issues in this report is based on a longer analysis in a Commission staff memorandum: Joshua Weiner, "Deinstitutionalization and the Problem of Mental Hygiene," 1975, which summarizes the history in New York State.

2. Larry Sutton, "Gifts Open Doors to Medipatients," *New York Daily News*, December 3, 1981, p. 9.

3. See, for example, the collection edited by Ethel Shanas and Marvin Sussman, *Family, Bureaucracy and the Elderly* (Durham: Duke University Press, 1977). This volume has quite a different emphasis than Shanas and Streib's 1965 collection, *Social Structure and the Family: Generational Relations* (Englewood Cliffs, N.J.: Prentice-Hall). The earlier book, to which Sussman contributed, was a sort of manifesto for what I've called the unimpaired extended family position.

4. George Ross Fisher, *The Hospital That Ate Chicago: Distortions Imposed on the Medical System by Its Financing* (Philadelphia: Saunders Press, 1980).

5. 1981 Harris-National Council on Aging survey, reported in Harris and Associates, *Aging in the Eighties: America in Transition* (New York, 1981). The item was, "There are a number of ideas about long-term health care for the elderly. Please tell me whether you strongly approve, approve, disapprove, or strongly disapprove of the following changes . . . 'Medicare, the health insurance program for the elderly, should cover more health care services provided at home.'" Eighty-seven percent approved or strongly approved.

6. Health Care Financing Administration, *Long-Term Care: Background and Future Directions*, Discussion Draft, Office of Policy Analysis, HFCA 81–20047 (Washington, D.C.: Health Care Financing Administration, 1981), p. 25.

7. Ibid.

8. 1981 Harris-National Council on Aging Survey, *Aging in the Eighties*. The item was "Families that provide health care at home for the elderly should be given a tax break."

9. U.S. Office of Management and Budget, *Budget of the United States for Fiscal Year 1983* (Washington, D.C.: Government Printing Office, 1982), pp. 5–130.

10. Karen Davis, "Equal Treatment and Unequal Benefits: The Medicare Program," *Milbank Memorial Fund Quarterly (Health and Society)*, 53, 1975: 449–488.

Notes

11. Ruth S. Hanft, "Health Manpower," in Steven Jonas (ed.), *Health Care Delivery in the United States* (New York: Springer Publishing Company, 1981): 126–168.

12. Steven Jonas, "Ambulatory Care," in Jonas, *Health Care Delivery in the United States.*

13. A search for experimental models similar to this proposal indicated that Health Care Financing Administration experimentation with HMOs in Medicare had been remarkably limited, considering Medicare's great size and cost. The Fallon Clinic in Worcester, Mass., however, succeeded in securing a Medicare waiver for prepaid benefits for 6,000 patients and reduced hospitalization by its members to an average of 2.5 days in place of 4 for other elderly in Worcester County. Difficulties, however, were encountered with some local doctors who complained that the clinic was "stealing" their patients. See Robert Reinhold, "Competition Held Key to Lower Medical Cost," *The New York Times,* April 1, 1982, sec. A, p. 1.

14. 1981 Harris-National Council on Aging survey.

15. Ibid.

16. Thomas C. Hayes, "Panel Suggests a Retirement Age of 68 for Social Security Benefits," *The New York Times,* November 19, 1980, sec. A, p. 20.

17. A Harris Survey reported in James Jorgensen, *The Graying of America: Retirement and Why You Can't Afford It* (New York: McGraw-Hill, 1980).

18. Warren Weaver, "Europeans' Pensions Rely on General Funds," *The New York Times,* January 17, 1982, sec. A, p. 21.

19. Among the total public, 56 approving to 26 disapproving; among the elderly, 46 to 27. 1981 Harris-National Council on the Aging survey.

20. Leonard Silk, "Economic Scene," *The New York Times,* October 30, 1981, sec. D, p. 2.

21. President's Commission on Pension Policy, *Interim Report* (Washington, D.C.: Government Printing Office, November 1980).

22. U.S. Senate, Committee on the Budget, *Tax Expenditures: Relationships to Spending Programs and Background Materials on Individual Provisions* (Washington, D.C.: Government Printing Office, 1978).

23. Charles Robert, "The Hot Potato Syndrome," *News of Action in Our Community, Special Supplement* (Hempstead, N.Y.: Nassau Action Coalition, April–May, 1979).

24. The extent to which Social Security depresses individual savings rates has been the subject of heated debate among economists. Martin Feldstein in "Social Security, Induced Retirement, and Aggregate Capital Accumulation," *Journal of Political Economy,* 82, No. 5, 1974: 905–926, argued from time series analysis that Social Security halves personal savings and causes a 33 percent reduction in total personal and corporate saving. Feldstein later extended his empirical analysis to data from 15 capitalist countries with similar conclusions: see Martin Feldstein, "Social Security and Private Savings: International Evidence from an Extended Life-Cycle Model," in Martin Feldstein and Robert Inman (eds.), *The Economics of Public Services* (London: MacMillan Press, 1977). Others have argued that any negative effect on savings is much smaller. One such argument is in Michael R. Darby, *The Effects of Social Security on Income and the Capital Stock* (Washington, D.C.: American Enterprise Institute, 1979). Robert Barro argues that the Feldstein model ignores family intergenerational transfers which might take place in the absence of Social Security, and that

Notes

models adjusted for this show little negative effect of Social Security on savings; Robert Barro, *The Impact of Social Security on Private Saving: Evidence from the U.S. Time Series* (Washington, D.C.: American Enterprise Institute, 1978. A summary of several empirical studies in the literature on this issue, concluding with dissent from Feldstein's position, is Louis Esposito, "Effect of Social Security on Saving: Review of Studies Using U.S. Time-Series Data," *Social Security Bulletin*, 41, No. 5, 1973: 9–17. See also George von Furstenberg and Burton Malkiel, "The Government and Capital Formation: A Survey of Recent Issues," *Journal of Economic Literature*, 15, 1977: 835–878, for a summary of the literature, and Alicia Munnell, "Private Pensions and Savings: New Evidence," *Journal of Political Economy*, 34, 1976: 1013–1032, for empirical arguments in support of the Feldstein position.

25. Martin Feldstein, "Toward a Reform of Social Security," *The Public Interest*, 40, Summer, 1975: 75–95.

26. Speech at Graduate School of Business Administration, New York University, 1975, reported in John J. Tarrant, *Drucker: The Man Who Invented the Corporate Society* (New York: Warner Books, 1980).

27. A number of case studies have described the emergence of strong and rewarding mutual-help networks in age-dense housing. A classical sociological description is Arlie Hochschild, *The Unexpected Community: Portrait of an Old Age Subculture* (rev. ed.; Berkeley: University of California Press, 1978). See also Irving Rosow and Frances M. Carp, *A Future for the Aged* (Austin: Texas Press, 1966).

28. See Rosow and Carp, *A Future for the Aged.*

Appendix

TABLE 1

Estimates and Projections for the Age
Composition of the Population, 1900–2040

| Year | % of Population 65+ | | | | Median Age | | | |
| | Actual (Est.) | Projection under Fertility Assumption:* | | | Actual (Est.) | Projection under Fertility Assumption | | |
		High	Mid	Low		High	Mid	Low
1900	4.1				22.9			
1910	4.3				24.1			
1920	4.7				25.3			
1930	5.5				26.5			
1940	6.9				29.0			
1950	8.2				30.2			
1960	9.3				29.5			
1970	9.9				28.1			
1980	11.2				30.2			
1990		11.7	12.1	12.6		31.4	32.8	33.7
2000		11.3	12.2	12.9		32.5	35.5	37.3
2010		11.1	12.7	13.9		31.1	36.6	40.2
2020		12.7	15.5	17.8		31.4	37.0	41.7
2030		14.0	18.3	22.1		31.2	38.0	43.2
2040		12.5	17.8	22.8		30.7	37.8	43.9

* High assumption = above replacement level
  Middle assumption = at replacement level
  Low assumption = below replacement level

SOURCE: Beth Soldo, *America's Elderly in the 1980s, Population Bulletin*, 35, No. 4 (Washington, D.C.: Population Reference Bureau, 1980), Table 2, p. 9, derived from U.S. Bureau of the Census, *Historical Statistics of the United States: Colonial Times to 1970* and "Projections of the Population of the United States: 1977–2050," *Current Population Reports*, Series P-25, No. 704, 1977.

Appendix

TABLE 2
Percentage in Families among Widows in Households, 1960–1980

Year	65–74	75+
1960	50.1	59.9
1968	37.7	50.6
1969	37.3	50.6
1970	35.5	45.0
1971	32.1	43.7
1972	31.3	40.4
1973	33.9	39.4
1974	32.7	39.3
1975	31.5	38.3
1976	29.1	36.9
1977	27.3	37.6
1978	27.4	35.9
1979	27.5	33.2
1980	26.5	33.4

SOURCES: U.S. Bureau of the Census, *Census of Population: 1960, Persons by Family Characteristics,* Final Report PC(2)-4B, 1964; "Marital Status and Family Status: March 1968," *Current Population Reports,* Series P-20, No. 187, 1969; "Marital Status and Family Status: March 1969," *Current Population Reports,* Series P-20, No. 198, 1970; "Marital Status and Family Status: March 1970," *Current Population Reports,* Series P-20, No. 212, 1971; and annual reports on "Marital Status and Living Arrangements" for each March, 1971 through 1980, *Current Population Reports,* Series P-20, Nos. 225, 242, 255, 271, 287, 306, 323, 338, 349, and 365.

TABLE 3
Work Force Participation

| | Percent of 65+ in Work force | |
Year	Male	Female
1950	45.8	9.7
1955	39.6	10.6
1960	33.1	10.8
1965	27.9	10.0
1970	26.8	9.7
1975	21.7	8.3
1980 (projection)	20.1	8.0
1990 (projection)	16.8	7.5

SOURCE: U.S. Bureau of the Census, "Demographic Aspects of Aging and the Older Population in the United States," *Current Population Reports, Special Studies,* Series P-23, No. 59, 1976.

TABLE 4

| | Poverty Status of Persons 65+ by Race, 1959–80 | |
Year	White	Black
1959	33.1	62.5
1967	27.7	53.3
1968	23.1	47.7
1969	23.3	50.2
1970	22.5	48.0
1971	19.9	39.3
1972	16.8	39.9
1973	14.4	37.1
1974	13.8	36.4
1975	13.4	36.3
1976	13.2	34.8
1977	11.9	36.3
1978	12.1	33.9
1979	13.2	35.5
1980	13.6	38.1

SOURCE: U.S. Bureau of the Census, "Money Income and Poverty Status of Families and Persons in the United States: 1980, Advance Data From the March 1980 Current Population Survey," *Current Population Reports,* Series P-60, No. 127, 1981.

220

Appendix

TABLE 5

Poverty Status by Race and Living
Arrangements, 65+, 1967 and 1975

Group	Poverty Rate 1967	Poverty Rate 1975	% Change (Relative)
Black	53.3	36.3	31.9
Male	51.4	31.0	39.7
In Families	47.6	23.6	50.4
Unrelated	61.6	51.8	15.9
Female	54.7	40.2	26.5
In Families	40.8	24.2	40.7
Unrelated	80.8	65.8	18.6
White	27.7	13.4	51.6
Male	21.3	9.5	55.4
In Families	17.6	6.9	60.8
Unrelated	41.9	23.8	43.2
Female	32.4	16.1	50.3
In Families	18.2	6.4	64.8
Unrelated	57.2	29.1	49.1

SOURCE: U.S. Bureau of the Census, "Characteristics of the Population Below the Poverty Level: 1975," *Current Population Reports*, Series P-60, No. 106, 1977.

TABLE 6
Approval of Coresidence, 1973–78

	% "Good Idea"
Size of Place	
less than 10,000	31.7 (2,206)
10,000–50,000	32.7 (2,146)
100,000–1 million	34.9 (1,221)
greater than 1 million	39.7 (446)
Race	
White	31.9 (5,328)
Black	43.5 (632)
Other	52.4 (42)
Religious Preference	
Protestant	31.1 (3,836)
Catholic	37.5 (1,525)
Jewish	25.6 (121)
None	37.8 (442)
Other	47.5 (80)
Area of Ethnic Origin	
Puerto Rico	71.0 (38)
West Indies	47.9 (19)
Mexico	47.3 (93)
Africa	44.7 (257)
Eastern Europe	34.4 (411)
Western Europe	32.1 (1,787)
English-speaking countries	28.9 (155)

SOURCE: Secondary analysis of General Social Survey for 1973, 1975, 1976, 1978.

TABLE 7
Coresidence Approval by Cohort by Year*
% "Good Idea" with "Depends" Excluded

Cohort	0	1	2	3	4	5
Age in 1957	—	21–29	30–39	40–49	50–59	60+
Approval in:						
1957	—	33.4	30.5	35.1	35.0	26.4
1973–75	41.1	36.5	32.2	27.9	26.9	25.7
1976–78	48.9	47.2	37.0	29.3	25.2	22.6

* These are not panel data: the cohorts represent different individuals but from the same birth years at different points in time.

SOURCE: Secondary analysis of 1957 Health of Older People Survey and General Social Surveys for 1973, 1975, 1976, and 1978; see chapter 3, notes 9 and 13.

Appendix

TABLE 8
Financial Help by Race, 65+

Group	Financial Help to Children	Financial Help from Children	"Income" from Children or Other Family Member	Primary Income Source from Relative
White	45.8% (1,642)	19.9 (1,649)	3.7 (2,239)	.6 (2,162)
Black	41.7 (300)	49.9 (300)	8.0 (478)	1.5 (457)
Hispanic	42.9 (49)	42.7 (49)	4.0 (60)	1.0 (60)

Bases are different because of different numbers of exclusions; the first two items are based only on respondents with living children. Bases from weighted sample are adjusted back to reflect approximate actual numbers of elderly whites and blacks in sample.

Source for tables 8–13: Secondary analysis of 1974 Harris-NCOA survey of the Aged, 1957 baseline from tabulations from NORC-Shanas Health of Older People survey. See chapter 3, notes 13 and 25.

TABLE 9
Financial Help by Living Arrangements, 65+

Living Arrangement	Percentage Receiving Help
Alone	25.0 (510)
Head with Children	37.1 (151)
Head with Other Family	14.4 (628)
Wife of Head	33.8 (470)
Relative of Head Parent or Other	49.9 (138)
(minor categories omitted)	

TABLE 10
Financial Help by Income, 65+

Income	Financial Help to Children	Financial Help from Children	"Income" from Children or Other Family Member	Primary Income from Relatives
$0–3,999	37.0 (839)	33.2 (841)	4.3 (1,141)	.2 (1,127)
$4,000–6,999	46.8 (566)	17.6 (566)	4.0 (769)	.9 (738)
$7,000+	58.5 (545)	12.7 (548)	3.9 (752)	.9 (735)

223

TABLE 11
Financial Help by Age and Occupation

	Provide Help	Receive Help	Help with Food	Income from Relatives	Primary Income from Relatives
Age					
65–74	47.9	22.0	6.9	3.0	.6
	(1,288)	(1,294)	(1,758)	(1,779)	(1,708)
75+	42.1	23.1	13.0	6.0	.8
	(744)	(746)	(1,008)	(1,013)	(989)
Occupation					
White collar	51.8	12.4	6.5	3.0	.7
	(491)	(493)	(745)	(752)	(727)
Blue collar	44.4	25.8	8.6	3.9	.6
	(948)	(948)	(1,232)	(1,243)	(1,194)
Farm	37.7	25.4	14.7	5.1	.4
	(241)	(241)	(297)	(299)	(294)

TABLE 12
Financial Help Attitudes

	% Specifying Children as Appropriate Income Source
Race	
White	10.9 (3,572)
Black	6.3 (425)
Occupation	
White collar	12.6 (1,387)
Blue collar	9.1 (1,943)
Farm	16.8 (161)
Place	
Central City	9.3 (1,338)
Suburban	8.1 (1,137)
Town	6.0 (653)
Rural	16.0 (1,128)

TABLE 13
Financial Help Attitudes by Cohort,* 1957 and 1974

Cohort	Age in 1957	Age in 1974	% Specifying Children as Appropriate Income Source 1957	% Specifying Children as Appropriate Income Source 1974
0	—	21–37	—	13.3
1	21–29	38–46	63.1	11.5
2	30–39	47–56	59.8	9.5
3	40–49	57–66	56.0	5.7
4	50–64	67–81	39.6	6.6
5	65+	82+	36.4	6.6

* "Cohorts" from repeated cross-sectional surveys.

TABLE 14

The Shift from Mental Hospitals to
Nursing Homes, 1960–1970

(Numbers in Thousands)

Group	1960			1970			% Change in Rate
	Number	% of Elderly	% of Institutionalized Elderly	Number	% of Elderly	% of Institutionalized Elderly	
Number of 65+	16,560	100	—	20,066	100	—	—
65+ in institutions	615.1	3.7	100	971.6	4.8	100	29.7
In nursing homes, personal-care homes, homes for the aged	388.0	2.3	63	795.8	4.0	82	72.4
In mental hospitals	177.8	1.1	29	113.0	.6	12	−52.4
In other institutions	49.2	.3	8	62.9	.3		5.2

SOURCES: Urban Institute, "Nursing Home Supplies and Demands, 1964–1974" (Technical Proposal, June 20, 1975); U.S. Bureau of the Census, Census of Population: 1960, Persons by Family Characteristics, Final Report PC(2)-4B, 1964; Census of Population: 1970, Persons by Family Characteristics, Final Report PC(2)-4B, 1973.

TABLE 15

Actual and Projected Growth of Selected
Federal Pension Expenditures
(in Billions of Dollars)
Actual through 1980, Estimates and Projections for 1981–86

Year	Military Pensions	Civilian Pensions	Social Security*
1972	3.9	3.8	39.4
1973	4.4	4.5	48.3
1974	5.1	5.6	54.9
1975	6.2	7.0	63.6
1976	7.3	8.2	72.7
1977	8.2	9.5	83.9
1978	9.2	10.7	92.2
1979	10.3	12.4	102.6
1980	11.9	14.7	117.1
1981	13.8	17.6	138.3
1982	15.6	19.9	159.6
1983	18.4	22.5	180.9
1984	20.4	25.2	201.3
1985	22.3	27.8	221.6
1986	24.2	30.3	242.0

* Includes disability pensions. For 1981, estimated expenditures for Old Age and Survivors Insurance were $119.4 billion.

SOURCE: Office of Management and Budget, *Budget of the United States for Fiscal Year 1982* (Washington, D.C.: Government Printing Office, 1981).

Appendix

TABLE 16
Selected Tax Expenditures, 1981–83
(Millions of Dollars)

Description	1981	1982	1983
Net exclusion of pension contributions and earnings:			
—employer plans	34,230	36,695	37,885
—plans for self-employed and others (IRA and Keogh)	3,660	5,030	5,820
Exclusion of Social Security retirement benefits	9,105	10,130	10,595
Exclusion of Social Security survivors' and dependents' benefits	1,785	1,935	1,975
Exclusion of Railroad Retirement benefits	370	375	375
Additional tax exemption for the elderly	2,250	2,355	2,370
Tax credit for the elderly	130	135	135
Exclusion of veterans' pensions	95	85	90
Exclusion of capital gains on home sales for persons age 55 or older	600	635	820

SOURCE: Office of Management and Budget, *Budget of the United States for Fiscal Year 1983, Special Analysis G,* Tax Expenditures (Washington, D.C.: Government Printing Office, 1982), Table G-1.

INDEX

Index

Index